SAPPER
FROM WALES

A SOLDIER'S LIFE

SAPPER
FROM WALES

A SOLDIER'S LIFE

Kevin Roberts

DEDICATION

To the memory of my best friend and old Army buddy,
"Allen Kilcullen"

Al sadly passed away in 2012, aged just 43. He always remained healthy and extremely fit throughout his 22 year army career. A light drinker, and a non-smoker he was still banging out 10 milers a couple of times a week, even after he left the military.

Originally from Scotland, he settled in Wales with his wife Sue, (who I introduced him to during the 90s) along with his son, Thomas, and stepdaughter, Kimberley.

He landed himself a dream job soon after, operating large cranes in Holland. During a routine medical examination a dark spot was revealed on his lung; the result was devastating - he was diagnosed with lung cancer and passed away 8 months later.

During his time in the Corps of Royal Engineers he served in Germany, Northern Ireland, Norway, the Balkans, and deployed on operations to the Gulf as a qualified advanced military diver during Op Telic.

As well as a qualified Skill at Arms and Map reading instructor, he was Commando trained and loved to compete in the Army biathlon competition annually in Bavaria. A truly consummate professional, he also completed the gruelling month-long SAS selection course in the Brecon Beacons, which shows the calibre of man he was.

On Remembrance Day every year I raise a glass and shed a tear to all those service personnel and veterans who have served our country with pride and honour.

"Rest in Peace old Friend"

During the editing of this book, We received shocking news that my brother, Christopher, who inspired me, and guided me towards joining the Royal Engineers, died suddenly after a tragic accident at his home in Thailand.

"Rest in Peace Bro"

CONTENTS

Part 1

GROWING UP

Born in the summer of 1969 in the small, picturesque town of Llangollen in North Wales, I am the youngest of four sons and was brought up in the small village of Corwen which nestles along the banks of the river Dee, midway between Llangollen and Bala.

A great place to grow up during the 70s where all the families and kids knew each other, and we all went to the same school. I was fortunate enough that my uncle drove the school bus and he often used to let me sit next to him on the ledge at the top of the front steps, something which would be severely frowned upon today, and rightly so. He drove us from Clawdd Poncen, a small suburb roughly a mile away to town.

On a recent visit down memory lane, I was showing my kids where the school used to drop us off at the bottom of the hill by the old Midlands Bank, and we had to walk the rest of the way up a steep hill to the school at the top. They couldn't believe kids as young as five years old had to walk up such a steep hill, which made me chuckle, but I was saddened to see the old school had been flattened and was now a housing estate.

The community was close knit and folks there looked after one another. Growing up, those summers seemed long, our days spent playing in the surrounding fields and in the small communal park - not fenced off like the parks today, and no rubber matting to protect you when you fell. The swing frames would wobble from side to side as you swung and the ground below the seesaw was hollowed away from years of children's feet scraping the soil away. The hollow scrapes would often fill with water and turn muddy when it rained and our parents used to play bloody hell at us when we got home, school shoes soaked and muddied.

As a child I was forever getting hurt, falling off the swings or spinning too fast on the merry-go-round, and I would end up going home battered and bruised. One particular mishap when I was about six years old ended up with a trip to Wrexham hospital. I was playing on the slide and I followed a chubby kid impatiently down before he had the chance to get off. As I slid down after him he was still trying to get off at the bottom. I went flying down after him and gave him a kick up the arse shouting,

"Yes, got you," before he lost his balance and sat back down on my left arm, now resting on the side of the slide.

The pain was excruciating and unlike anything I had ever experienced before. Holding my arm, I ran home screaming. I was rushed to hospital where the X-rays revealed that my arm had been broken in two places, and a plaster of paris cast from the top of my fingers around my thumb, all the way up to my armpit, saw me out of action for the rest of that summer.

I loved being outdoors in all weathers, playing team games like cowboys and Indians, or cops and robbers, chasing each other around the estate, hiding in alleyways and people's gardens to evade being captured by the pursuing team. British bulldog was also a favourite of mine and every kid in the estate would gather in the playing field to take part. The older kids would decide who would be the bulldog as the rest of us lined up along the edge of the field. With the nominated bulldog standing in the middle, we would have to run the length of the field and within the boundaries, identified with jumpers and t-shirts laid out along the edge, the aim of the game being to reach the other side without being tagged by the bulldog. Once tagged, you would link hands with the bulldog, and with each pass the bulldogs defensive line grew longer, stretching across the field and making it more difficult to run past without getting tagged. The outstretched line would pull one way then the other, and you would have to time your run to coincide with a gap opening on your side of the field, to sprint past and avoid getting caught.

Unfortunately, all these games now seem lost in a child's imagination in this modern digital age, and the crazy world of technology we now live in. I never owned a watch as a child, my natural body clock never let me down once; the rumble in my stomach told when it was time to eat and the whiff of home cooking in the air confirmed it was time for dinner. All the kids on the estate would Instinctively all run home and throw a hot meal down our necks before rushing back to the playground for a game of hide and seek. My brothers used to tell me it was time for me to go home as it was getting late, I used to reply,

"The streetlights aren't on yet," was soon followed by a quick kick up my backside.

Most households only had one television and anyone who owned more was considered to be well-to-do. Changing channels was an effort - you had to get up out of the chair and press a button, or turn a dial like an old transistor radio, to tune in to another station. The well-to-do families had the state-of the-art remote-control system, a long lead attached to a control box allowing them to flick through the 3 channels from the comfort of their armchair, great if the remote-control lead wasn't ripped out by someone walking past, tripping over the lead, and pulling the cable from out of its socket on the front of the television set. Television was more for grownups in the evenings and by the time I got in from a full day of running around I would fall asleep usually squashed between my brothers on the couch, or I would just crash out on the bed. The only time I would watch television was if the weather was too bad to go out, or on a Saturday morning I loved watching the likes of Laurel and Hardy and Tarzan.

Dad was a linesman and during the winter months he was forever out. He would be on standby, always being on callout to fix the power lines during the cold winter nights. Blackouts were a common occurrence and my mam used to make sure there were always plenty of matches and candles in the drawers for such events. Mam was a part-time insurance collector, and she would drive around the local villages collecting people's pension and insurance money for the Prudential. My brother, Michael, is the eldest of us brothers, followed by Christopher, then Martin, with yours truly being the baby of the family.

Household incomes were tight, and most families had to adapt and find alternative ways to put extra food on the table. Dad used to poach salmon from the river, and snare rabbits and shoot pheasants, ideal for making stew for a bunch of growing lads. He also helped other dads to fix their cars and liked to tinker with engines, especially motorbikes. He loved watching the Isle of Man TT racing in the 50s before he had us lot. I only found out about this a few years ago whilst visiting him in his care home just a few months before he died, when he was suffering from dementia. We were sitting in the communal room watching the 2015 Isle of Man TT racing on the television. I knew he was keen on motor-racing so I struck up a conversation, thinking it would end up in a repetitive dialogue of nonsense, and those who know will be able to relate - dementia is a cruel disease of the brain, and those suffering from it will repeat the same stories over and over again. But, I was taken aback when he started to tell me of his early days when he was part of a motorcycle club in Llangollen during his late teens and early twenties, he spoke vividly for over an hour of his annual visits over to the Isle of Man. He went on to tell me how he would save his money and a group of them from the club would go on their motorbikes to Liverpool and board the ferry. He even told me he did a lap of the circuit on his own 500cc motorcycle; I forget the make that he told me, but my mam later confirmed it was all true, even dusted off an old photo album and showed me the black and white photos of him on his bike over on the Isle of Man.

From an early age I knew I wanted to be a soldier. I used to sometimes watch black and white cowboy films when the weather was too bad to play outside, and war movies in technicolour on a Sunday afternoon, often acting out battle scenes on the landing of the stairs with my small, green, plastic soldiers. The Vietnam War dominated television at the time and my fascination for war games developed as I grew older. My friends and I would team up in pairs and run around the woods holding a branch as a weapon and sneak up on one another, seeing who could shoot who first. I had no fear of heights and I used to climb high up into the trees to gain the upper ground on my unsuspecting mates. I would look down and see them wandering aimlessly around the woods in search of me, before shouting,

"We give up, where are you?" and seeing the look of surprise on their faces when I shouted down from high up. They used to call me mad, and when I look back, I think I was, but it built up a resistance to heights for what lay ahead later in my life.

One Christmas morning when I was about 6-years-old, I woke up early. Martin and I shared a bed and weighed down with 4 heavy duty blankets before the days of luxury quilts. At night, mam used to tuck us in so tight we had to wriggle up towards the pillows to escape. I looked down towards the end of the bed, and there was a brand-new drum set. This was the first new toy I had ever had - all my previous toys were hand me downs, and being the youngest of four, you can imagine how battered and used they were by the time they got to me. I was so excited I started playing. Martin was the first to wake, telling me to shut up as it was too early and still dark outside. I should have listened! Michael, now of an age for booze, and like a bear with a sore head, came steaming into our bedroom, put his foot through the bass drum, snapped my drumsticks and tossed the cymbal like a flying saucer out the window. My short lived drumming career was over, so I was forced to revert back to playing with my less noisy little, green, plastic figures, still dreaming of the day I would become a soldier.

Martin and I were forever having pillow fights, jumping up and down on the bed, smacking each other around the head. One evening before bedtime, thanks to our efforts, the wooden bed frame snapped, and worried we would get into trouble, Martin had a brainwave. He lifted the snapped frame precariously back into position. Snickering, we shouted for Michael to come upstairs to challenge the two of us to a duel, knowing full well we would get our heads caved in, but Martin's idea was ingenious and worth a beating. After several loud cries Michael took the bait and came running up the stairs. We quickly jumped onto the opposite side from the snapped bedframe and waited for the drum-smashing hooligan to arrive. He jumped on the bed with an almighty crash.

"Yes, we got you," I mumbled to myself.

"Mam, Dad" we both shouted, "Michael's broken the bed".

Oh the sweet taste of revenge was blissful, as he got a clip around the ear.

I was given a hand-me-down bike for my birthday, complete with several layers of fresh paint which made it look as good as new. I wedged a wooden lollipop stick in the back wheel to make a rattling noise against the spokes as I rode which made it extra cool in my eyes; the whole street used to know I was on my bike and mam used to get complaints off the neighbours when I was riding up and down at 06:00 in the mornings. It became my signature calling card and my friends would come out and meet me.

As we were riding around the field by the old chapel one day we came across a wasp nest, a small hole in the side of the bank along the hedge line. We watched for a minute or two as the wasps flew in and out of the hole before deciding to throw stones, as you do, trying to see who could get a stone in the hole. Turned out it wasn't the best decision we ever made. Talk about stirring up a hornets' nest! Wasps started flying out of the hole and attacked us from all directions, as we waved our arms, trying to get away. I was stung on the top lip, I ditched my bike and ran home screaming. My lip was swollen like a balloon, and again I was rushed to hospital as by now my face had swollen so much my eyes were almost shut. The Doctor considered me to be very lucky; he said if it had stung me lower on my face the reaction could have caused my throat to swell and I may well have choked to death. Not sure if this was true, or his way of telling me to stay away from wasps' nests in future. Either way it worked and to this day I'm still wary when I see a wasp hovering too close. My friends joked that it was too early for me to be wearing my Halloween mask.

Skateboarding was the new craze, and no sooner had I recovered from my temporary facial disfigurement, I got the speed wobbles going down Corwen hill. The hill is long and steep, and I soon discovered skateboards are not equipped with brakes and I was not wearing any protection. I fell off, and with a split head and road-rash all down one side, it was back to Wrexham hospital for some stitches to my head and some sticky plasters for the cuts.

Mam was getting fed up with running me in and out of hospital, she even had to rush me to the surgery one day when my pee turned red. The doctor looked in my mouth, saw that my tongue, and even my teeth were also red and quickly diagnosed the beetroot juice I drank from the jar earlier to be the root of the problem.

In 1977 we left Corwen and moved to Denbigh. I was a happy kid and quickly made new friends. I would go out early on weekends with my new friends, climbing trees and exploring the castle grounds. We would also alternate camping in each other's gardens and go scrumping apples throughout the night, bringing bags of apples into the house. In the morning, mam would say,

"Hey! don't get caught stealing them, you little buggers", and in her next breath would tell us, "make sure you steal some pears next time!".

It kept the family going on apple and pear crumble for a while.

Grease, the hit musical film was now showing in the cinemas and was a huge success, portraying rock'n'roll American high schools during the 50s. Our little gang decided to call ourselves the "T" birds, after the main gang portrayed in the film. My parents couldn't afford to buy me a leather jacket, so I had to make do with an old red corduroy one instead. I tried to emulate the "T" bird's logo on the back, except my eagle looked more like a dysfunctional sparrow, and my blue suede shoes were a pair of brown trainers. We thought we were the coolest gang on our estate.

My school days were also a bit hit and miss, as I played truant all the time. I hated being confined in a classroom and used to bunk off school a lot. Mr Jinks was the school ratcatcher, a retired policeman who knew all the hiding places. He would catch me most days somewhere around the castle grounds and would order me to get back to school.

My favourite lesson which I never bunked off was Physical Education, and swimming was my favourite sport. My years in Corwen swimming pool made me a good swimmer. The Head of Physical Education was a man we all knew as Charlie Oscar. He looked older than the other teachers with white hair, and was feared by every boy in school. Rumour had it he was a sergeant in the army during WW11. After PE we would all have to shower; everything was communal and the teacher would sometimes walk through the changing rooms to make sure we had all showered properly. If you were spotted with dirt on you, he would send you back into the showers. We would always be messing about in the changing rooms, and I mastered the art of towel flicking, but it bloody hurt like hell when you got spanked with the end of a wet towel.

Charlie was doing his usual rounds, making sure we had showered properly and caught me towel flicking. In one swift movement he grabbed my curly hair with two fingers, the bit just in front of my ear, and lifted me up on tiptoes, it was Charlie's signature move. As he marched me through to his office while I was still butt naked, rollocking me as we went, I knew this wasn't going to end well. He had a leather sole off an old shoe which he named Oscar, and slapped me right across the back of my leg. The boys in the changing room next door could hear the slap and everyone went quiet as soon as they heard me scream, it was 5 times more painful than any towel flick - you knew you were in the shit if Charlie got a hold of you.

Our family still had close ties in Corwen, and we would often go back and visit family and friends. It was there that I attended my first funeral - Dylan was a soldier serving with the parachute regiment and was killed by the Provisional IRA in an ambush in Northern Ireland along with 17 other British soldiers. It was the same year my brother Christopher joined the Welsh Guards. I was 10 years old when we travelled to Pirbright for his passing out parade; they looked so smart in their red tunics and bearskin hats. Prince Charles, now of course King Charles III, was in attendance as he was the Colonel of the Regiment at the time, and during the post parade lunch he walked up and down the tables greeting the families. He asked me if I enjoyed the parade, and if I wanted to be a soldier.

I looked up at him and said,

"I hope so".

He smiled at me and said, "Good lad".

Tension between Argentina and Britain over the Falkland Islands was brewing and in 1982 Argentina invaded the islands. Christopher was being deployed with his battalion, and we, together with thousands of other families, made our way to Southampton to wave farewell as they set sail aboard the Queen Elizabeth 2, a huge cruise liner capable of carrying thousands of passengers. The government had commandeered it to ferry the allied troops to Ascension, a small volcanic island in the middle of the Atlantic ocean, halfway between Britain and the Falklands. There the troops were to be disseminated onto various Royal Navy frigates, destroyers and landing craft. The crowds numbered in their thousands on the dockyard as we all waved and cheered; for some it would be the last time they would see their loved ones.

The next few months were pretty tense. My big brother was at war. As I watched the intensity of the scenes of conflict unfold on the news, I realised that this was no longer someone else's war, or a movie I had watched a few years earlier - it was our war and it was very real. I watched in horror as HMS Galahad was attacked and struck by an Argentine Exocet missile, the images of the ship engulfed in smoke and flames. We knew the Welsh Guards were onboard and could see the life rafts coming ashore. We stared at the television in the hopes of catching a glimpse of him, but were devastated to soon receive the news that he had been killed during the attack. For 3 days we were in mourning until we received a phone call -someone apologising for what is known as a clerical fuck up! A monumental mistake to inform a family they had lost a loved one, we were now being informed he was alive and well and was not even on board the HMS Galahad when it was struck.

When Christopher was away my uncle Len used to sleep in a single bed opposite the bunkbeds where Martin and I slept. He would come home drunk and snore the roof off. Fed up with it, Martin decided to buy a couple of small plastic guns which we loaded with small ball bearings and kept under our pillows. One dark night Uncle Len snuck into the bedroom around midnight as usual after the pubs had closed, consciously trying not to wake us - but we were armed and ready! Five minutes later he was sucking the roof in with his snoring and making sounds which belonged in a zoo. Martin peered down from the top bunk and said,

"Ready".

Gun already in the firing position we both unloaded a volley of shots into his back. It felt so satisfying, but unfortunately only meant a brief pause in his overture and then we had to resort to putting tissue in our ears to try and drown out the noise.

The following morning, he was wondering where the hell all the ball bearings had come from as we both acted all innocent. Little did I know, Martin was funding our nightly battles with the beer change he stole from Uncle Len's blazer jacket pocket he would hang on the back of the chair.

Uncle Len was a kind and funny man who would always give me money for sweets. He was a builder and I remember he took me on a job once re-felting a flat roof high up on a big house. Health and Safety would have had a field day - no railings, no scaffolding, in fact no safety gear at all. I had no fear, as my days climbing castle walls and trees made me fearless of heights. But sadly soon after that he was involved in a car accident on his way to work. A car was overtaking, coming towards him. They had a head-on collision, and he died a few days later in hospital. I would have put up with his snoring for many more years just to have him back.

As teenagers, my mates and I would often gather in large groups at the top of the town, and go and spend what pennies we had in the pinball café. One evening the gang decided to go glue sniffing in the quarry - it was all the rage back then. I hated the thought of it but went along anyway. They were all busy sniffing away and getting high when the local bobby, a special constable, caught us and rounded us up. He took all our names and sent us on our way. When I got home I got a clip around the ear! The special had been to my house and informed my parents that I had been sniffing glue and up to no good. No matter how much I pleaded my innocence, I was always going to be guilty.

My parents divorced when I was 15 years old. It was a tough time for all of us, but all my brothers were older, and I was in my last year of high school. My mam rented a small house, more like a cabin, about 5 miles away in the country. Isolated, I soon learned to drive the car up and down the country lanes. She even allowed me to drive the 5 miles each morning to school; pulling up outside the school gates at the age of 15 in her 1.3L Triumph Dolomite was cool, even if the car was yellow.

Soon enough my school days were over, but I decided to wait until I was 18 years old before going to the army careers office. This meant marking time for the next two years. After a short time in the cabin with mam, I moved in with my dad and Martin, as he now had his own place in town. Martin was nearly always working away though, so it was mostly just me and Dad at home.

Shortly after moving in with Dad in 1985, I enrolled on a Youth Training Scheme (YTS) as a welder, a scheme introduced at the time to get school leavers off the streets and gain a trade, as unemployment in the country was high. l worked 40 hours a week sweeping floors, painting metal beams, and making cups of tea for the other workers. Attending college once a month our instructor would ask what we had learnt at work since last month. The answer was the same from all the students, we were all being used as skivvies and being taught nothing. Industries at the time, were owned and run by post WW11 businessmen who had the attitude of, 'get on with it and do as you're told'. That was just how it was, and we did get on with it.

Each morning around 10 am tea break, the butty wagon man would drive around the industrial estate selling sandwiches and sausage rolls out the back of his old Morris Marina van. It had 2 wooden makeshift shelves which he would slide out to display his goods, a bit of a 'Del boy' trader with everything being on tick until payday. On Friday, just prior to our break, the boss would hand out our little brown envelopes with our wages in cash, as he knew we all needed to pay the butty man. And bang on cue, there would be the butty man waiting with his van doors shut, and his little black book in his hand, expecting payment before starting the weekly cycle all over again.

My weekly bill would amount to around a fiver - a quarter of my weekly wage. Then there'd be another fiver to dad when I got home for my keep, leaving me around a tenner for the pub that night. Bitter was 5p cheaper than lager, at 68p a pint, which meant I could get rat-arsed and still have enough for a bag of chips and some scraps from the local chippy on my way home.

Saturday morning Dad would wake me up to see if I wanted to go to the pub for a few pints. It was a bit of a ritual, because he knew I was skint. I think he just wanted to hear my lame excuse before he would give me a tenner to see me right - champion!

After eight months of painting metal beams with red lead and sweeping floors and not having held a welding torch once except for my days at college, I decided to jack it in for a more lucrative job, stacking shelves in Kwik Save Superstore. The guys there were a great bunch, most of whom I was in school with or knew from the pubs. My wages doubled from 50p to around £1 an hour. I was now able to get a Chinese takeaway on a Friday night instead of scraps from the chippy.

Kwik Save was the main shopping hub for the town, and I knew most of the customers who shopped there. I was busy filling the shelves one afternoon when I heard someone calling out my name from the other aisle. As I bent down to look between the shelves where the voice was coming from my work colleague and a good friend, Andy Evs, Sue's brother, was pointing a jiff lemon in my direction, squirting it right in my eye. As I stumbled back an elderly lady was passing and I knocked her shopping trolley flying. Blinded, and with no sympathy from the elderly lady who then complained to a member of the management team, I was called into the office to explain myself. I came up with some lame excuse so as not to grass up my jiff-lemon wielding colleague and I received a verbal warning for my efforts.

A revenge attack was on the cards! I planned my move, and some days later, I lay in wait for the perpetrator to enter the stock room. I was armed to the teeth with two jiff lemons ready to unleash a volley of shots. The stockroom had lots of trolley cages full of stock which made for good cover to hide behind. The large heavy plastic doors with plastic clear windows (for seeing through to avoid any collisions when pushing the big heavy pallets) allowed me to identify my target approaching. As he approached I ran and hid ready to ambush him. I heard the distinctive slapping noise of the heavy plastic door open, then shut, and I waited a few seconds more before hearing his footsteps getting louder and closer into the kill zone. The moment of revenge had arrived. I jumped out and unleashed a volley of lemon juice. Damn! My revenge attack, although satisfying, was witnessed by a red coat! A member of the management team had followed him through the doors, which I had failed to spot when he approached the stock room doors. And that's when I received my second verbal warning,

I was now treading on thin ice; two verbal warnings meant my next offence would certainly be a sacking, so I decided now was the right time to visit the army careers office and pursue my calling.

I was sent on a 2-day army selection camp to Sutton Coldfield near Litchfield in the West Midlands. Young lads from all over the country, all with their own different aspirations, rocked up, some wanting to join the Paras, others wanting to be Guardsmen, and the likes, but I was adamant I wanted to join the Royal Engineers. We were put through some tests which included fitness, basic maths and English, followed by a medical assessment by a military doctor, including the old cough and drop examination.

"Drop your pants," he said, rubbing his hands, as he proceeded to cup my balls in his hand. "Cough." This was apparently a medical examination to see if my balls had dropped, but just to make sure I asked one of the other lads if they had their balls felt.

"No mate," one of them said, the room fell silent for a brief moment before bursting into laughter when they saw the look on my face - squaddie humour had already begun.

Having successfully passed the army recruitment selection tests, I was invited back to Rhyl Army Careers Office on the 9 July 1987 and interviewed by the selection officer, and asked if I would like to accept service in the Royal Engineers. Thrilled, and filled with excitement I accepted and on that day I swore my Oath of Allegiance to Her Majesty the Queen, and was officially enlisted into the Corps of Royal Engineers.

My excitement grew more as I was handed a crisp ten pound note for my troubles and was given a reporting date of the 9th of August, exactly a month later, and told to collect my train ticket before my departure. The ten pounds I received was spent celebrating at my local pub, the Masons Arms in Denbigh.

A month soon flew by and as I boarded the train at Rhyl, my parents waved me farewell, something they had done 8 years previous with Christopher. Although divorced my parents remained friends and united in seeing their youngest son off, a proud moment, I guess, as they both had a tear in their eye as the train set off. It was only a few minutes into the journey when I remember feeling anxious and a sort of fear coming over me, and I soon started to question myself. Had I made the right choice? I felt worried and afraid, a feeling I had never experienced before as the realisation set in that I was now alone and I no longer had the protection of my family.

Part 2

BASIC TRAINING

Following the same route as the famous Welsh Dragon passenger train, which originally ran from Holyhead along the beautiful coastline of North Wales to London, I soaked up the tranquil views and the quiet and peaceful part of this historic journey before arriving at my first stop, Crewe in Cheshire. One of the world's most historical and significant railway stations, and serves as the gateway to the North of England.

A mad dash over the bridge to the opposite platform for the train to London, and a few hours later I arrived at the busiest train station in Britain, Euston. I disembarked and followed the herd of people into the underground, not really knowing what, or where the hell I was going. I paused, trying to work out the colour coded rail network of the underground whilst being jostled by fellow travellers. I eventually found the platform I needed for the next leg of my journey. Standing on the platform breathing in the stale smell, which was being forced through the tunnels by the trains as they moved about in the underground labyrinth, suddenly my train appeared screeching and clattering out of the darkness. As I watched it pull to a halt, a voice from the speaker system blurted out those words so synonymous with the London underground - "Mind the Gap". The gap was big enough a polar bear could have fallen between. Thankfully, nowadays the trains are lower, narrowing the gap between the platform and the train.

The doors opened and I squeezed myself in for the short ride to Kings Cross and back above ground. The last leg of my journey and 5 hours after leaving Rhyl train station, I finally arrived at Aldershot, the home of the British Army - a journey thousands of young men and women have done before me, regardless of cap badge or corps, and who had no doubt carried with them the same emotions.

I stepped off the train and standing there on the platform to greet me was an army corporal dressed in military uniform, creases running down the front of his trouser legs as sharp as a samurai sword, and boots so shiny you could see your reflection in them.

"Excuse me mate, I'm Kev," I said. "I'm here to join the Royal Engineers". There was a brief pause as steam began emanating from his ears.

"Mate...mate! Do I look like your fucking mate," as he pointed to a coach parked up outside the station, already half filled with a bunch of sorry looking lads like me.

I boarded the coach; it was silent as I plonked myself down in an empty seat and waited amongst the other passengers. A short time passed, a few more sorry looking lads boarded and all the while I was feeling like I was wanting to get off and go back home. Too late, the Corporal stepped on and with a quick headcount, instructed the driver to set off. The coach journey was around 20 minutes, and we all sat in silence, probably all thinking the same thoughts - "What the fuck am I doing here". You could also feel the anxiety amongst us as we arrived at the gates of Gibraltar Barracks and pulled up next to our allocated accommodation block. No sooner had the coach driver applied the handbrake, the corporal stood up and we received our first set of snap orders,

"Get off the bus and form up in 3 ranks over there," he ordered, pointing over to an open area of ground.

"What about our kit?"

More steam began to emanate as I sensed he was holding back slightly, biding his time, knowing full well he would be getting his claws into us soon enough. We were greeted by more smartly dressed corporals and a sergeant, as we formed up in 3 ranks and briefed on some dos and don'ts, who's who, and what's what. He informed us we were about to receive a grand tour of the camp so we could orientate ourselves with our surroundings. Great idea, I thought, half expecting to step back onto the coach. Then I looked across to see the coach driver was busy unloading our baggage and laying it neatly in one long line along the kerbside. A corporal then stepped forward, dressed in the clothing only issued to physical training instructors - boots, lightweight trousers, and a blue tracksuit top. The sergeant finished his brief and handed us over to him.

"Right you lot, when I give the order to march, you march, and when I give the order to double time, you jog at my pace, do you understand?" he said.

This was followed by a variety of positive responses - "Yep", "Aye", "OK".

His demeanour suddenly changed and we were soon corrected with, "You address me as Corporal". This was repeated, only this time with a bit more authority, "DO YOU UNDERSTAND," as we all immediately responded in unison "YES CORPORAL".

Pleasantries over with, he set us off marching down the road like the bunch of undisciplined misfits that we were, and soon gave the order to break into double time. We were all pushing and shuffling as we tried to get into step with the man in front to avoid kicking each other's heels. For me all I could think about for the whole 30 minutes we were doubling around the camp with the corporal pointing out the various facilities like the NAAFI shop, barbers, gymnasium, Quartermaster's stores, drill square, telephone boxes, guard room, and finally the training area, was why the bleeding heck did I bother buying a pair of new shoes specially for this day. They rubbed like hell, I hadn't even started training and I already had blisters. I'm sure my thoughts at the time were emulated across all the new recruits that afternoon. What the hell have I let myself in for, and did he really need to show us the training area.

Back at the accommodation block we were allocated a bed space within a four-man room. I was allocated bedspace number 3 on the right next to the window as my home for the next 10 weeks. Tired, sweating, and ready for a rest we were marched over to the QM's stores to sign for our bedding. I queued with all the other recruits in one long line outside the QMs bedding store and waited to be called in to collect my bedding. One pissed stained mattress, four itchy heavy-duty blankets, a fire retardant over sheet, two stinking pillows and some clean sheets, folded up in half in the mattress. I carried it in front of me, arms stretched around and gripping my hands as tight as I could, struggling to see in which direction I was walking with a piss stained mattress squashed against my face. We looked like a bunch of ninja turtles with our shells on back to front, wandering aimlessly around the camp trying to find our accommodation block.

The first evening was spent in briefings, and being issued uniforms, before being informed that we would be having a room inspection at 06:00 hours the next morning. "You are to clean the ablutions, polish the floors, your military uniform hung and ironed neatly in lockers, bed blocks made, windows cleaned and bins emptied."

How the hell are we supposed to get all that done by 06:00 hours we all thought? I tried getting up at 04:00 hours to stand a chance of getting ready, but all to no avail - I was still looking like a bag of shit. Other nights I tried staying up late until 02:00 and having a wash and shave before getting a couple of hours sleep. We had to ensure the ablutions were spick and span and our beds were made and a bed block construction of folded sheets and blankets placed at the head of the bed (which took ages to perfect) with our brasses and buckles polished and laid out on the mattress and this meant that most nights were spent sleeping on the floor. It took me a while to figure it out, but I soon realised whichever way I tried, I stood no bloody chance of getting ready on time, and the lack of sleep soon took its toll.

"Stand by your beds," came the Corporal's voice bellowing down the corridor.

You could hear the shuffles from the other rooms as last-minute adjustments were being carried out before the Corporal entered our room.

"Room, Room, Shun," warned the recruit nearest the doors whose job it was to bring the room to attention whenever a corporal or above entered a room.

He passed the threshold and took one look at the small metal bin and brush which was neatly placed by the side of the door, and said in that tone of voice - the one with pauses in between each word, the tone which tells you you're in the shit type tone - "What... the... fuck.. is that!" pointing to a minute piece of fluff in the bin.

The recruit nearest answered nervously, "It's a piece of fluff, Corporal". "You're a fucking minger," was the corporal's response. "Yes, Corporal," he replied as the corporal instructed him to place the metal bin over his head, and march up and down the corridor, and shout repeatedly, "I am a minger," "I am a minger," whilst hitting the bin with the broom handle.

The urge to laugh was overwhelming, which landed us all doing press ups for the remainder of the inspection.

Several more cock-ups that day resulted in an evening of quick-change parades, a form of discipline designed to deter any future mishaps. It provides an evening of entertainment for the corporals and a form of punishment for us known in the military as a beasting. We paraded in front of the main training staff's office and that served to remind us that cock-ups cost lives. We were being punished as a reminder before being given two minutes to get to our rooms and changed into a uniform of their choosing, and back on parade ready for inspection. It was never their intention to inspect us, as they knew we would look like a bag of spanners. After several mad scrambles through the corridors and changes into every uniform in our lockers, my entire military uniform issue now lay strewn all over the floor. After exhausting all the dress codes we had in our lockers the evening finished off with the corporals instructing us to dress in a uniform not recognised in the military dress code, the old mess tin order! Butt naked we had to place 2 mess tins on a webbing belt around our waists, with one dangling at the front and the other dangling over the crack of our arse. We looked like a tribe that had just wandered out of the Amazonian rainforest.

The final words of the evening - "Room inspection at 06:00 hours," - the bastards!

Our day-to-day uniform was known as works dress: black boots, green lightweight trousers, a green itchy shirt, and a camouflage baseball style cap, which identified us as 'pongos' - new recruits still in basic training. Basically, It was a target indicator for every Tom, Dick and Harry to have a pop at you. We had to march everywhere with our arms swinging shoulder high and there were eyes everywhere waiting to pounce. The moment you let your guard down and relaxed, a window would be lifted, or a door would fly open, and some twat would be screaming his head off at you to sort your shit out, and threatening you with some bullshit punishment, so to avoid any conflict I just ran everywhere. Even the young officers would get on the band wagon and use any method to show their newfound power. I couldn't even take a shit in peace without someone wanting to yank my chain.

I was on guard duty at the front gate one morning when a young officer approached the gate on foot from Minley Manor where the Officers' Mess was situated, just across from the main camp. I recognised him but was instructed by the guard commander to check all ID cards before letting anyone onto camp, so I stopped him and asked,

"May I see your ID card please sir?"

He kindly obliged, showed me his ID card before placing it back in his wallet. He then looked at me and said,

"So, what's my name?".

Bollocks! I'd only looked at the picture and he took great delight in reporting me to the Guard Commander. I spent my next break doing press ups in the cell.

Payday was every fortnight, and we would form up in 3 ranks outside the office. Our troop sergeant would call out our names in alphabetical order, on hearing your name, you would bring yourself smartly to attention, fallout and march into the office, halt in front of the paymaster's desk, salute and state your name, rank, and number. Being a Roberts I was one of the last to be called; my assumption at this point was that all the other recruits called before me were either in their bed spaces counting their cash, or in the NAAFI having a sneaky beer. My assumption was soon shattered! When my name was called, I smartly came to attention and marched into the office, feeling pretty confident about my ability to perform the perfect drill manoeuvre. However, I mistimed my step and kicked the paymaster's desk. Before I could salute I was being screamed at by one of my training corporals.

"Get out that door you useless fuck."

And quickly marched down the corridor and into the quadrangle, a hollow concrete space between the accommodation block, about the size of a small courtyard, enclosed inside the building. There I was confronted with all the other recruits who went before me. There were guys in press up positions, others doing burpees and some in the stress positions. I guess they never mastered the perfect drill manoeuvre either! Payday was postponed for another day.

The drill square became a daily event, with the drill instructor barking orders to turn one way and the odd recruit turning the other, resulting in hours of marching up and down the square. We also received some remedial pay parade drill, until finally we got paid. The paymaster handed over my wages and gave me some bollocks speech about the Queen running out of money. There was a jar on the side of the desk which I clocked, full of tenners. He took pleasure in reminding me about the ten pounds I had received when I swore my Oath of Allegiance, and she would now like it back, stating very clearly, those of us who didn't donate their tenner would find themselves back in the quadrangle. If only the queen knew her money went towards funding their piss up at the end of our 10 weeks' training!

Many an hour was spent on the drill square, with my most memorable moment being nothing to do with learning or practising drill, but having to show-parade my bed space and bed layout on the square. During morning room inspection, a fly landed on the table nearest to me just at the moment our corporal entered the room. As the fly landed next to me, I got both barrels.

"Roberts, what the fuck is that?" he said.

By now the fly had disappeared and I replied, "It was a fly, Corporal".

Due to my obvious reply, he proceeded to unload a barrage of spit in my face, with my punishment for the fly intrusion being a show parade at 18:00 hours that evening on the drill square. Whilst the rest of my troop headed for the cookhouse for dinner, myself and a few other unfortunates were busy running backwards and forwards with room furniture, positioning it on the drill square as per our room layout: bed, bed mat, bed block, table and uniform all laid out ready. I stood nervously awaiting my corporal's arrival, and a few moments later he came marching over, looking like he wanted to kill me. I brought myself to attention.

"So, where is he?" he screamed.

"Who, Corporal?" I replied.

"The fucking fly, who do you think? You bloody imbecile"

Basic training is designed to break you down, then rebuild you into a more disciplined and robust individual so the system can turn you into a soldier. It's stressful, and individuals can sometimes crack under the pressure. One recruit in the opposite training party to ours received a letter from his girlfriend back home informing him that she had met someone else, a term commonly referred to in the military as a 'Dear John' letter. News of this type plays heavily on a soldier's mind and they will often keep it bottled up inside for fear of ridicule. Eventually they will snap, and this recruit decided to throw himself out of his second-floor window during morning room inspection, almost killing himself. Unfortunately, the 'Dear John' letter dates back to the times of the trenches in World War 1 and it can have a devastating effect on a soldier's morale, including fellow soldiers within their unit. I have witnessed this far too many times over the years, including the effect it had on myself.

Passing out parade loomed, marking the end of basic training, and a proud moment for 5 Troop, 55 Training Squadron, to show our families and friends we were no longer useless teenagers and that we had passed the British army entrance test.

Preparation for the big day began as we set about ironing our uniforms, polishing our brasses, and bulling our boots with several layers of boot polish until the shine was clear enough you could see your own reflection. We would also dry clean our rifles to remove any excess oil previously applied to prevent any rust spots forming. The last thing you want is to drop your weapon during a drill movement and look a right tit in front of your family.

The big day was now almost upon us. There was a hurricane brewing out in the Atlantic, later to become known as 'The Great Storm of 1987', but the legendary BBC weather forecaster, Michael Fish, played down its likely severity to the nation during his weather report; despite the met office warnings, he simply said, "It will be breezy in Spain". The next day we were hit by an extra tropical cyclone, causing an estimated 2 billion pounds' worth of damage across Britain. It was said to have been the worst storm to hit our shores in 300 years. We set about on a major clear up mission to clear the roads leading up to camp, as well as the parade square and the camp itself ready for our big day.

Families arrived safely and were greeted with tea and coffee before being seated in the small grandstand which had been erected by the side of the drill square. We began the day by conducting various military demonstrations, a section attack across the square with lots of smoke and blank rounds being fired simulating an attack on an enemy position, was soon followed by a physical training display with telegraph poles being thrown around, before we changed into our best uniform for the final parade. As we all scrambled to quickly into our best kit, the penny dropped - the punishment show parades we received a few weeks earlier were not just a punishment, they were designed to prepare us for this day. Marching around on the drill square knowing the eyes of our loved ones were watching our every move did fill me with enormous pride. It was probably best that the mess tin order did not form part of the parade on such a proud occasion.

After a few days leave it was time to start 10-weeks of Combat Engineer training, this time wearing a beret and cap badge, and no longer needing to swing my arms shoulder high. The days of running everywhere to avoid someone jumping out of the bushes to catch me for not marching properly seemed in the distant past.

Combat Engineer training is diverse and teaches the Corps fundamentals: mine clearance, handling explosives, bridge construction, water crossing and defence fortification. The bullring situated on the Minley training area, designated for detonating small explosive charges, was a circular cutting inside a woodland surrounded by trees and was heavily sign-posted as a danger area. Plastic explosive, sausage shaped and weighing roughly half a pound and wrapped in white paper with the initial PE4 stamped in bold black letters, denoted it as Plastic Explosive type 4. We were each handed a stick and instructed to unwrap the paper and discard it in the bin bag provided for proper disposal, due to explosive traces. We were then ordered to mould it like playdough into a tennis sized ball. Ball-shaped explosive in hand we lined up and were instructed to walk in single file through the narrow opening in the trees and into the bullring. I led the first group of ten down the opening through the trees and we formed into a semi-circle, spaced a few metres apart facing inwards towards the instructor. Placed on the ground in front of us were a few items which I recognised from our classroom lesson earlier, as the parts when assembled would make up the detonating device: a length of detonating cord, safety fuse, a detonator and a grip switch. The instructor gave us a safety brief - never run or panic when dealing with explosives. Each length of safety fuse was cut at slightly different lengths; he explained, mine being the shortest would detonate first and the last man who entered the arena being the longest would detonate last. We assembled the pieces together and went live, inserting the detonator into the explosive and waited for the order to fire the switch. Together we all released the safety and clicked the trigger mechanism on the grip switch, the fuses were now ignited. We were then ordered to calmly remove the grip switch. Hands trembling like recovering alcoholics we turned and faced the way we had entered and started to slowly walk out. It soon dawned on me that I had to walk past 9 other explosive charges with their fuses now burning! We made our way out of the bullring, and as I walked through the treeline, bum cheeks firmly clenched, the explosive charges began to explode at five second intervals - for such a small charge they made a very loud bang.

The Jackson Club was our place of safety, a haven and the one place on camp where you could go without some corporal screaming down your lug-hole. It was run by a Christian faith group originally founded by a Miss Daniells in 1863, and today it is renowned for its cheesy beans on toast, which every sapper since its doors opened on camp back in the 70s, will know.

Combat Engineer training complete, we were all now officially Wedgeheads, an expression dating back to when the Royal Artillery ran away in the Crimea, forcing the Engineers to rescue their guns before the Russians stole them. In the chaos, dead infantry officers' bodies were used to wedge the wheels to stop the cannons rolling down a hill. Each individual within my training party was sent on to their chosen field; most went to Chatham to the Military School of Engineering to become tradesmen, electricians, plumbers, bricklayers and the likes, the signallers went to Chattenden, which was also in Kent, to learn how to become bleeps, and I remained in Gibraltar Barracks to become a driver.

The military driving school was based not far away in Church Crookham, and those of us who remained would be coached down every morning after breakfast.

I went on to gain the licences I needed to drive Heavy Goods Vehicles. As well as gaining my HGV licence I also learned vehicle parts recognition and how the combustion engine worked, before going on to service and maintenance the various vehicles - all vital knowledge needed to go on and become a qualified specialist military driver. As I already held a car licence, which very few of my training party did, it allowed me to advance quicker and I was the first of my party to gain my HGV licence and went on to join my first unit in the spring of '88.

Part 3

FIRST UNIT

With my fully loaded VW polo, ironing board included, I set off around the M25 and up the M11 towards Cambridge, Atlas Road map and route card sitting on the passenger seat with handwritten directions to Waterbeach. I was still only 18 years old and had hardly set foot out of Wales, let alone driven. I was full of nerves but also excited to see what adventures lay ahead. My heart started pounding as I drove up the short stretch of road, lined with black and white kerb stones, to the front gate - I had finally arrived at 39 Engineer Regiment. I was directed up to the guardroom where I pulled up, got out of my car and casually strolled up to the hatch with a sign above it - all visitors report here. The hatch opened, and I showed my ID card and asked if I could book in and have a permanent car pass. It happened to be the guard commander who saw me, and he asked me which field unit I had just come from, probably thinking as I owned a car I was posted in from Germany.

"I've just come straight from training, mate," I said, thinking I'd now got my big boy pants on.

My reply was met with a slight pause, followed by a death stare as his attitude towards me suddenly changed;

I sensed he was vexed as he booked me in. He directed me to the 48 Field Squadron (Construction) office and told me to report to the squadron sergeant major. I made my way over there and booked in with the sergeant major's orderly corporal, who told me to take a seat and wait. A few minutes later a large built, middle-aged man walked in, dressed in his NBC suit with camouflage cream on his face.

He greeted me with, "Who the fuck are you?".

"Er, Sapper Roberts, sir," I replied, shitting my pants as he looked like a grumpy old fucker.

He walked around and sat behind his desk and told his orderly to make him a brew before turning his attention over to me.

"So, where you posted in from?" he asked.

"I'm straight out of training, sir," I replied.

"Well get the fuck out of my office, and march in properly then, shall we?" he bellowed.

Not needing to be told twice I leapt up from the chair and shuffled quickly out of his office, took a deep breath and marched straight back in and halted smartly in front of his desk. Oh no! I thought. I had seen that look before and knew what was coming my way.

"Get to the guard room," he said and off I sprinted where I was met by my old mate from 5 minutes early, grinning from ear to ear. He had obviously just received a phone call from the sergeant major as he ordered me into the courtyard.

"Pick up the shell," he ordered.

In the courtyard was a large artillery shell conveniently placed in the corner and a 20-minute beasting ensued. He took great pleasure in reminding me that he wasn't my mate, and to stand to attention in future when the sergeant major enters the room. It was at that moment my excitement and dreams were shattered. I soon realised I was just a sprog, fresh out of training, and for the next six months I'd have no mates and I would still be treated like a recruit. Bullying was rife and I soon learned to keep my head down until the next poor bastard came along.

The camp was previously an RAF station during World War II, which made it ideal for the regiment's specialised war role - ADR (Airfield Damage Repair). Our mission was to repair bombed airfields in support of the Royal Air Force during times of war. The old disused airfield was perfect for carrying out dry training. We would dig up the old runway to simulate bomb damaged craters and practice filling them in and capping them to allow the runway to remain functional. Every year around June time the squadron would deploy over to RAF Gutersloh in Germany for two months. The Harrier GR3 jump jets stationed there provided a sense of realism to training, vital during the cold war threat from the East. As part of the transport section, I would drive across with the road party as part of the convoy via Harwich to the Hook of Holland ferry crossing, and the main body of troops from my squadron would fly direct from RAF Brize Norton. We boarded for the overnight crossing and headed straight to the bar. Two pints in and there was an announcement over the tannoy system informing us of our delayed departure. A cheer was raised from all the drivers as we instinctively knew this meant an extra few more beers could be drunk and with a few hours extra in bed the following morning. News soon broke out of a bomb scare, and the ferry captain asked our officer in charge if we could carry out a search of the ferry. The boss refused and explained to the captain that we were not Explosive Ordnance Device (EOD) Specialists - a specialist branch of the Royal Engineers. As we were travelling in uniform the civilians on board soon caught wind of the situation and were up in arms, demanding to disembark, and they began to voice their anger towards us. Our seniors quickly ushered us back to our cabins and told us to remain inside so as not to cause anymore angst amongst the civilian passengers.

Bored soldiers couped up in a small cabin is not always the best idea, and is a sure recipe for disaster. The duty-free bottles of whiskey soon appeared along with a deck of playing cards, and by midnight the ferry was host to a dozen or so naked squaddies doing the conga, singing "we are, we are, we are, we are the Royal Engineers" our corps' favourite song, usually only heard, bellowing out from the confines of the Naafi bar and mess halls - not on the decks of P&O ferries. Fortunately for us it turned out the bomb scare was a hoax and our delayed departure of 12 hours meant extra time to sober up before the long drive ahead.

Drinking in the military is part of our culture, and those not hardened to the drink would find themselves waking up having slept in their own vomit and then some! A general once said, "Our Soldiers need a war. They're getting lazy," and I think he was right. Soldiers would often wake up having had an eyebrow removed or half their moustache shaved and replaced with a drawing of a penis in permanent black marker pen during their incoherent state. You would often hear a soldier shouting out, "for fuck's sake," once he had looked in the mirror and realised he had been 'Rolfed', followed by chuckles from the rest who still lay in their beds, some shouting "Can you guess what it is yet?" a phrase once used by the famous Australian artist of the day. Our sergeant major was not amused at seeing his soldiers on parade with phallic symbols being displayed on now red raw, but comical, unsightly faces. He would soon restore law and order by imposing the threat of an alcohol ban. The threat worked and soon put a stop to Rolf's antics.

Airfield Damage Repair training meant long days out on the airfield. RAF Gutersloh was a very active runway, with Harrier jump jets constantly taking off and landing. It was the back end of the cold war and RAF Gutersloh being the most easterly UK airbase station in Germany was Britain's first line of defence against an aerial attack from the former Soviet Union. With fast jets constantly taking off and landing, patrolling the sky's overhead and even with our ear protection, the noise was deafening, and the smell of jet fuel constantly lingered in the air. Training was conducted on a large concrete area just off the main runway with two to three large craters used to simulate a bombing raid of the main runway. Training intensified and the base moved into exercise conditions. Sirens sounding over the speaker system, and a voice calling out the words, "Red, Red, Red" meant an air attack was imminent, small explosive charges would be detonated simulating the runway being bombarded, adding realism to the exercise. Troops would don their respirators during the bombing raid as a precautionary measure, as chemical cluster bombs were a real threat from the soviets. We would run for cover into the aircraft hangers, followed by a soak period of around 30 to 60 minutes before deploying the Nuclear, Biological and Chemical (NBC) sentry to carry out a chemical drill test to determine if it was safe to remove our respirators. Only when the order, "All clear, all clear" sound was given was it assumed safe to remove our respirators.

Reconnaissance teams would deploy out into the airfield to assess the damage, clearing any unexploded ordnance, before reporting back their findings to the Officer Commanding and Sergeant Major. Movement within the aircraft hangar began to stir, a sure sign we were about to move out, as we waited inside the hangar with its huge steel doors and earth covered roof, able to withstand a direct hit from a 1000lb bomb. The large steel hangar doors began to wind open, and we were given the signal to start our engines; it was time to go to work. I drove a 15 tonne tipper and my vehicle was loaded with aggregate ready to backfill any bomb craters we needed to repair. A plant operator in a large Terex, with its 5 tonne bucket would be the first vehicle to deploy, backfilling the rubble now strewn all over the runway into the crater. As myself and the other tipper-driver would reverse to top up the hole with extra aggregate until the crater was filled slightly higher than the level of the runway, the dynamic compactor would roll up and begin to drop its 5-tonne weight up and down, compacting the aggregate until it was almost level with the surface of the runway. The other tipper driver and I would be hooked up at either end of a large screed beam, and in unison we would drag it across the crater, like a filler knife smoothing over Polyfilla to fill a hole in a wall, except on a grander scale using heavy plant machinery to smooth the aggregate. Once smoothed over and any excess stone cleared away our crane operator would lift the large Bomb Damage Repair Mat off the trailer I had parked to the side of the runway earlier. This would lower into place at the side of the crater, and a team of soldiers waiting in the back of a 4 tonne Bedford truck would be radioed in to roll out the large mat over the crater, essentially capping it. Using specialised power tools they would bolt it to the concrete before grabbing their bass brooms, and in one long extended line would sweep the mat clean of any foreign object which could be potentially sucked up into a jet's engine and cause a catastrophic engine failure.

Saturday night in the Naafi bar was known as stomp night, a military term used for a disco, and the boys would often pile on the dance floor and carry out their mat sweeping dance. Lining up and pretending they had a brush in hand they'd start sweeping the dance floor including those dancing. It was an inside joke which was funny to us but met with confusion to outsiders as to why a bunch of drunk squaddies were trying to sweep them off the dance floor, and often the odd slap would raise a cheer.

We departed from RAF Gutersloh and headed back to blighty with a ridiculous amount of cheap alcohol and cigarettes stocked up over the last 2 months. Our precious cargo was now safely stowed away in every compartment of my vehicle: I had cigarettes hidden behind seats, in tool bins and hidden in the cargo I was carrying, and I would pray that the "monkeys," (the Royal Military Police) didn't spot check me, as they often did prior to departure. My lame excuse was that in the event of being caught I was to act dumb - they do say to play to your strengths! I have no idea how it got there and would have certainly landed me in the shit along with my fellow drivers. The beer I kept for myself, and the cigarettes went on sale in my local pub back home in North Wales and made for a small profit;

they would ask when I was going back over to Germany for more supplies, and I was now in danger of becoming known as the local tobacco smuggler.

The journey back to Holland seemed much longer on the return than it did coming over. To break up the boredom on the long straight autobahns we would often swap drivers whilst on the move, 12 hours at 50 kilometres an hour is enough to send anyone mad. I would either jump behind the guy driving while he slipped to the side, or my favourite move was to climb out the passenger door and over the top of the vehicle cab and back in through the driver's door. I'd catch a glimpse of the faces behind the windscreens of the cars passing on the opposite side as they pointed with a look of disbelief. Lucky for me there were no mobile phones back then as I'm sure we would have been pulled over by the Polizei sharpish.

Adventure training at Capel Curig in Snowdonia next. As I detoured my military 4 tonne Bedford cargo truck I was driving up to my hometown of Denbigh with my oppo, my dad's face was a picture as I pulled up outside his house. After a quick pint in our local pub we arranged to meet the next morning at Llyn Brenig reservoir on the Denbigh moors for a spot of fishing. Dad had all the fishing gear and the next morning we met up as planned. My oppo, having never fished before, was keen to give it a go.

"Dad, where's the fishing gear," I asked, opening up the boot of his car.

"Oh shit," he said as he jumped back and drove the 7 miles back home to get it - in his excitement, he forgot to load up the fishing gear.

After a day on the lake and not a nibble between us, I wished he had just left his fishing gear at home. Snowdonia being my back garden growing up, I was able to showcase to my army buddies and even took them to Black Rocks Sands for a day on the beach, as well as rock climbing and canoeing in the best spots around Snowdon. They even met a few Welsh girls at the Swallow Falls club, near Betws-y-Coed.

To test the regiment's grit and resolve the Commanding Officer instructed his training staff to plan a 5-day arduous military competition, and in January 1989, he deployed his regiment to Thetford training area in Norfolk. The weather conditions were what you would expect for the time of year - cold and wintery, and the competition aptly named, 'Exercise Frosty Sprint' was put in motion.

Around thirty 8-man sections were formed to take part. Our kit packed and weapons drawn from the armoury, 2 sections - 16 men – were loaded up onto the back of 4-tonne troop carrying vehicles and transported to the drop off point, a large field being used as a holding area. There we waited to be called forward, a section at a time. The exercise was kept quiet from the exercising troops, a well-kept secret amongst the officers and senior non-commissioned officers (SNCOs) with only real time information being given out as the exercise began. So far we only knew our location.

The holding area began to fill up with more and more troops until around 300 soldiers were huddled close together. As the clear winter sky turned to night, a new moon meant only the cracked cyalumes hanging from the command tent gave any point of reference. Sections chatted amongst themselves whilst carrying out last minute adjustments to their kit. We waited in anticipation as a section at a time began to be called forward, and then disappeared into the dark night. The temperature was already hovering just above freezing, and eager to get moving our section was called to the release point. A set of orders and a grid reference was given to our section commander and we were off, carrying 40 lbs of combat equipment, with my self-loading rifle (SLR) held across my front.

"How far boss," I asked.

"I estimate around 20 km," he replied.

"Don't take the piss, How far really," I asked.

He paused for a minute, and together with our second in command (2i/c) he carried out a quick map appreciation after which our 2i/c pipped up,

"Nope, he isn't taking the piss. Heads down and arses up boys, let's get this smashed".

Frost had already started to form on our backpacks, and after several wrong turns and some rerouting through thick forests we finally arrived at our grid. It was around 2am, and a single cyalume hanging off a tent at the edge of a wooded area marked the spot where an SNCO was laid up in a small tent.

Checked in, he told us to bed down and report back at 06:00 for further orders. The cold now set in and I couldn't get my sleeping bag off my back quick enough before diving into it, but it offered very little warmth as I curled up in a ball, hand tucked between my legs and the cold barrel of my SLR pressing against my cheek, trying to keep warm. I must have only closed my eyes for what seemed like a couple of minutes, when the dreaded nudge followed by the words every soldier dreads,

"Kev, your turn for stag mate," my turn to stand guard while the rest of the section sleeps, I dragged myself out of my sleeping bag, the air was crisp, and a thin sheet of ice had formed on the ground, It was bitterly cold and my toes and fingers were numb, a quick session of jogging on the spot to get some life back into them, I was now able to break out my rations and fire up my hexamine burner to boil some water, for a hot brew. I woke the rest of the section and passed around mugs of tea with plenty of sugar which soon put life back into them, before shaking out and readying ourselves to report to the checkpoint SNCO, for our next set of orders.

Six other sections appeared from nowhere as we gathered around the small tent. It was still dark when the SNCO briefed us all.

"You will be faced with 6 stands today in the vicinity of this location. The stands will be both physically and mentally challenging. Each task will be timed, and each stand coordinator will score your overall performance".

Military skills including various engineering tasks, setting up and transmitting radio communications, battlefield casualty stands, log runs, and trailer pulls were some of the challenges we faced. Unbeknown to us at the time, each evening we would endure another gruelling night march of equal distance to the first. Each night got tougher, fatigue set in, and the night marches got slower, and seemed longer.

We had 2 guys from our section who had to drop out due to bad blisters on their feet and were unable to carry on. Other sections were losing men, too. It was time to dig deep and keep going. I felt myself weirdly getting fitter and strong as the days went on, even though my body ached, and my feet were sore. I suppose the thought of knowing lots of guys were dropping out who I imagined to be more capable than me, spurred me on and gave me that extra boost I needed to see me through. I began feeling a sense of pride, a sense of belonging as the week went on. Each day also involved at least one physical activity - a timed 5km log run - now on already tired legs. Any blisters I had were now ripped off. A change of socks and plenty of talcum powder and some heavy-duty sticky tape helped me get through the final night march; each step was painful, but

I made it to the end. I was now accepted as a fully-fledged member of the green machine!

Competition over and with a final hoorah from the CO and his merry band of officers, we came a not so disappointing 7th place, considering we were a slapped together section, made up of drivers and plant operator mechanics - the military's version of a civilian construction team.

With my confidence now sky high, I entered the regimental swimming competition, with each of the 4 squadrons battling it out in the pool. None of us were trained athletes; it was the equivalent of a high school gala event, beer bellies included, but I knew I was a good swimmer, and I was fit. I was now about to put my misspent youth in the swimming pool to the test. I plucked up my new found courage and confidence, convincing the sergeant major I was quick. Nobody had seen me swim before, so he took a chance and entered me into the breaststroke race. Having won that he then entered me into the butterfly race and before I knew it, the sergeant major was asking me,

"Is there a stroke you can't swim?"

"No sir," I replied.

"Good," he said. I've entered you into the medley, a race using all four swimming disciplines: backstroke, breaststroke, butterfly and crawl. This was going to test my abilities to the full, I thought, but I needn't have worried.

After winning all my races and becoming the sergeant major's new best friend for the remainder of the day, it was time for the medal presentation. The CO and his beautiful wife, a former model for Vogue magazine, arrived to present the prizes. Each time I was called up to collect my medal the cheers got louder, and as the former model gave me a peck on the cheek after going up to collect my third medal she remarked,

"You're a greedy one".

Regimental duties now loomed. It was time for sappers to go into hiding in fear of being nominated for a 6 month guard duty or a stint of waitering in the officers' mess.

Having already done my guard duty I felt pretty safe that I wouldn't get picked again. However as fortune had it ,and still in favour with the sergeant major, along with 6 others from across the regiment I was picked to be a lifeguard and sent on pool lifeguard course in Cambridge, in preparation for the summer opening. Devolved from all military activities for the next 6 months, working 2 shifts on a 1 week on, 1 week off rotation, 7-days a week - it paid to be a winner! It meant early starts, opening the pool for soldiers wanting to train before work, and then locking up late on hot summer nights, but we would take turns during our shift. One would do cleaning and maintenance, another would run the shop serving teas and coffees to the soldier's families, while the other kept a watchful eye over the children in the pool. During my week off I would travel back home to Wales. Friends and even family started to question if I was still serving , and to be honest I had it so good, I questioned it myself, but as they say, all good things soon come to an end and with the summer months over it was time to don the green skin and return to the normal duties of being a soldier.

Part 4

JUNIOR NON-COMMISSIONED OFFICER'S CADRE

In February 1990 at the age of 20, I was nominated to attend a Regimental Junior Non-Commissioned Officer's (JNCO) Cadre. My initial instinct was to decline the offer as I felt I wasn't ready, but after a talking to by my troop corporals I accepted the challenge, although somewhat reluctantly, I must admit.

The JNCO Cadre is a six-week leadership course, all soldiers must complete to kick start their career and to gain promotion to Lance Corporal. They say your first stripe is the hardest to earn and easiest to lose. I have seen many guys lose their first stripe, mostly due to alcohol and fighting. The CO has the power to bust you back down to sapper without a court martial, but it takes a general, usually a brigadier during a court martial, to strip a full corporal and above of their stripes.

The first week started off with some low level stuff, mostly polishing up on our basic military skills, map reading, first aid, weapon handling and some foot drill before we moved away from barracks and over to Thetford training camp, and away from the distractions of our parent unit. The moment we arrived the intensity immediately increased. The cadre staff began screaming and shouting as soon as we stepped off the coach,

"Right you lot, you've got 30 seconds to get your arses off this coach, grab your kit and get on parade".

Here we go again, the bullshit has started. We were ordered that for the duration of the Cadre we must always carry our military identification cards in our top left-hand pocket; I would normally keep mine in my wallet, as did most soldiers, it was easily forgotten when changing in and out of various uniforms several times a day - as I soon discovered. The troop staff sergeant shouted out,

"Show ID cards".

"Bollocks!" I knew instantly that I had left mine in my other shirt.

I scrambled to my luggage along with eight out of the 35 soldiers on parade who had also left theirs in their other shirt pocket. We were met with,

"What the fuck do you lot think you're doing?"

"Getting my ID card out of my shirt pocket, Staff."

And so a lap of the camp perimeter in double time for the lucky eight, was followed by, "The last one back goes again". Fortunately that unlucky sod wasn't me this time!

Having thought I had learnt my lesson on the ID card front, a week later during an evening room inspection

I again forgot to put my ID card in the top left hand pocket of my khaki flannel shirt, and was subjected to an hour's punishment with several other forgetful imbeciles. The beasting began with several laps around the accommodation blocks to get us blowing like hell, followed by a few press ups and burpees thrown in to get us really hot and sweaty. That was followed with a carrying of each other session around the now well-trodden circuit around the accommodation block, accompanied by a reminder that if we were seen to put the person we were carrying down, then the beasting would continue throughout the night - a bluff call, we hoped, but it was best not to take the risk! We made sure we didn't drop each other; the bastards had eyes everywhere. Fireman's carry, over the shoulder to baby-carry across the chest, followed by umpteen more press ups until our arms felt like lead, and they knew it.

We were then ordered to pick up empty 200 litre oil drums each and hold them above our heads. We were wearing combat helmets which left little gap between helmet and outstretched arms. They very quickly started shaking as they gave us a dressing down speech about the importance of having our ID cards in our possession at all times. Pausing for breath, the staff warned that if the barrel was to touch our helmet then it would be several more laps of the circuit. The speech droned on like a Shakespeare play as I felt my arms giving way, and then all hell broke loose, the barrel had supposedly touched the top of my combat helmet and the instructor got right in my face, yelling,

"You're a fucking weak individual Roberts, you don't deserve to be here". For a split second I saw red and threw the barrel on the floor. I knew at that moment he was right. He told me to pack up, but I refused to leave and picked up the barrel pleading with the instructor to let me carry on. I knew the last few weeks would have been for nothing and if I wanted any chance of getting promoted, I would have to do it all again. He sent the others away and continued to beast me for a further 10 minutes, trying to break me, but I was resilient and he allowed me to remain on the course.

Aspects of the JNCO Cadre is like basic training, polishing brass, bulling boots and ironing uniforms followed with some barrack room bullshit, which they say all makes for character building. I would love to meet the character who came up with that one!

Military lessons are a vital part of soldiering, and most of the lessons taught on the course were presented by us, the candidates. We would be marked on our presentation skills and the content of the lesson. No point in giving a lesson if no bugger understands what you're waffling on about; you have to be clear and precise. Lessons to be presented were allocated to us by the staff, and whenever we had free time which was of course premium time as they were on us all the time, we would use it to study in preparation. Supervised closely by the cadre staff, we were all given two presentations each, the first a 10-minute presentation of our choice, and the second a 30-minute military subject allocated to us.

For my 10 minute presentation I chose to fold an empty crisp packet into a small triangle, something I once saw a guy do in a pub back home in Wales. It dawned on me while everybody was eating their packed lunches, otherwise referred to as a nosebag, as it's the first thing soldiers do, is to stick their nose in the bag to see what it smells like before looking inside to see what delights were on offer. It was always the same shit - either a soggy tuna and cucumber or stale cheese and onion sandwich, a rubbery sausage roll, a caramel wafer biscuit and a pack of cheap and nasty crisps. I yelled out,

"Keep a hold of your empty crisp packets, fellas," and for the next few days I had crisp packets thrown at me from all directions.

I always get nervous when speaking in front of a class or a large group of people. I would get anxious, and my voice would tremble, and my body would shake; I always felt like I was being judged, and suffered terribly with stage fright.

As my career progressed, my confidence grew and a few years later, when I became a bridging commander, I was the subject matter expert and was soon carrying out many demonstrations, talking in front of large groups, including some very senior officers - I had finally managed to overcome my nerves and became more confident

Final exercise marks the final phase of training. We deployed out onto the 30,000-acre training area of Thetford, a locality I knew well from my last outing. It was time to put the leadership skills we had been taught over the last 6 weeks to the test. We weren't told the duration of the exercise, but we guessed it would be no longer than 5-6 days, as we needed to get back to Waterbeach and prepare for our passing out parade in front of family and friends.

Each of us set out carrying full combat equipment; the old issued 58 webbing was broken down into two parts: the first part was your Combat Equipment Fighting Order (CEFO) first issued to the British army in 1958, hence its cleverly adopted name - squaddies never have liked to over complicate things, keep it simple stupid. It was made up of a yolk strap clipped to your waist belt at the back, over your shoulders and clipped to waist belt at the front, several pouches would also be attached by metal clips that slotted into small holes along the edges of the belt: two pouches at the front contained three rifle magazines filled with 7.62 mm blank ammunition, a pouch on one side contained a full plastic water bottle and mug, a respirator pouch, a medical pouch containing basic medical supplies and 2 pouches at the rear containing 24hrs of emergency rations tucked inside 2 metal mess tins. Clipped underneath the waist belt and wrapped tightly inside was a bum roll, containing your Nuclear, Biological & Chemical (NBC) warfare suit. Packing it was like trying to squeeze a fat arse into a budget airline seat - it was a 2-man job, one to roll it up and kneel on it while another closed the strap, even harder when wet as the webbing would shrink slightly.

The second part was a large pack which you wrestled onto your back and clipped into the 2 loops which sat roughly in line with your chest. Its designers of the day must have been having a right laugh when they came up with its design and why it was ever called a large pack nobody ever knew, it was no bigger than a plastic shopping bag, and strapped to the top to complete the Complete Equipment Marching Order (CEMO) – was your sleeping bag and roll mat, the items you wanted to keep you warm and dry were strapped to the outside of your large pack like a big sponge soaking up the rain with a roll mat made of foam designed for extra comfort!

The clip attachments on the yolk were designed to be unclipped quickly during a contact; in a fire fight you could use your large pack as cover, resting your weapon across it whilst engaging the enemy. If you were being overrun by the enemy and you needed to make a hasty retreat, you could ditch the large pack and still be wearing your webbing containing your essential survival and fighting equipment.

Immediate action drill in a contact situation is to hit the deck, belly first, and make yourself as small a target as possible, then locate and engage the enemy. The section commander would almost immediately be screaming out if the enemy was not obvious to view, "Has anyone seen the enemy?" a standard command when incoming rounds can't be identified from source.

The reality is, once your down in the prone position, your bloody sleeping bag presses against the back of your helmet and forces your face into the ground, and one arm outstretched in front and pointing your weapon aimlessly, whilst struggling to unclip the damn large pack doesn't fill you with confidence if ever it was for real.

Fortunately, this was the last time I was to use the now outdated 58 pattern webbing, an experience only the old and bold of today have had the pleasure of. It was now being phased out and replaced with the new Personal Load Carrying Equipment 90 (PLCE). This newer issue would be more comfortable, hold more equipment, and could be thrown off one shoulder easily, when diving for cover. But for now, it was time to soldier on.

Each of us would also carry additional equipment in support of the section. The 84 mm Carl Gustaf anti-tank weapon, commonly referred to as Charlie G, was cumbersome, with an effective range against enemy tanks of around 350 to 400 metres. It weighed around 14kg and was carried in shifts amongst the section. Three anti-tank dummy rounds weighing over 3kg each also had to be distributed amongst the section and carried, as well as additional radio batteries weighing a couple of kilos each and the size of a motorbike battery. The Bren gun Light Machine Gun (LMG) weighs in at around 11 kg with its extra ammunition all added to the already heavy weight we were about to carry.

On the third day we were all pretty shattered, and it was my turn to carry the Charlie G. We had been patrolling all day and it was now dark. As we made our way through a dense forest, I stepped over a fallen tree and completely lost my balance due to tired legs and heavily overladen. I fell backwards, hitting the ground with a thump, with the wind taken out of my sails. I was unable to catch my breath as the section continued to march on, a couple of minutes passed and I was struggling to get back on my feet. Luckily the section realised I was missing and doubled back to find me laying there like a turtle stuck on its back waving my arms and legs in the air.

"Kev, what you doing fucking about," they chortled as they lifted me back to my feet.

"Just having a lie down. What the fuck do you think I was doing?"

Nobody was really in the mood for laughter at this point though, as we continued our course hoping for some respite soon.

I was placed in charge of our section and the next day I received a set of orders to patrol an area 10 km to the south of our present location; a small pocket of enemy fighters were causing havoc. I briefed the section on our mission and pointed out on the map the route we were to follow. After a few hours patrolling, smoke was spotted in a small clearing, and we went to ground, my section instinctively taking up a defensive position. Surveying the area for several minutes I decided to go forward and investigate. Tapping one man on the shoulder I whispered in his ear,

"You with me," and hand gestured to the rest of the section to remain in place.

They would give covering fire if needed. I moved slowly, crouching as I went forward, following the treeline, when I spotted two soldiers lying ahead. This was only training, but my senses were heightened and my adrenaline kicked in. I paused and questioned myself for a moment - what should I do? Should I shout a warning? Or do I engage? Are they friend, or foe? Fuck it, I thought, and I decided to chance it and ran at them unloading a full magazine of 20 blank rounds from my rifle. It wasn't real but felt good. What's the worst that could happen? If I screwed up I would get a rocket up my arse or another beasting from the staff, but in the end it turned out they were pleased with my actions, and I got my first well done in five weeks.

I was briefed at the scene. The smoke simulated an ambushed Land Rover which was now sitting in a nearby ditch, the scene was the result of the two enemy I had just eliminated. As there might be more enemy close by, we needed to act fast. The driver, I was informed, was dead and the passenger badly wounded. The guys set about patching him up and we recovered the vehicle and informed the staff we would drive him to the nearest field hospital, at which point they ended this phase of the exercise.

It was now day 4, and we could sense the exercise was close to the end. We would soon be home and dry, or so I thought. We had been briefed to patrol an area along the riverbank. As we approached a clearing by the water's edge we were met by our instructors. I could see a boat in the river, with a rope stretched tight across just above the surface of the water. It was now mid-February and still bitterly cold. I knew what lay ahead.

"Right fellas," one instructor said, "you have exactly 5 minutes to strip and waterproof your kit".

Quickly we wrapped all our kit except for our weapons inside our ponchos, a sheet normally used for making a shelter known as a 'basha'.

"Strip down to your knickers, fellas, and make sure nothing gets wet," our newly appointed section commander ordered.

He briefed us to have no more than two in the river at any one time to allow for the home bank to give covering fire in the event of an attack, and vice versa once we had bodies on the other side. The safety boat was downriver beyond the stretched-out rope in the event that someone got swept away, or cramped up in the freezing cold water, they could grab the safety rope or be rescued by the boat crew. I felt myself shaking uncontrollably as I entered the water, I was a member of the regimental swimming team, so the deep water didn't faze me. As I lay my weapon on top of my kit hoping I wrapped it properly so it would remain afloat, I took the plunge and went for it. The water was ice cold and I felt the blood being extracted from my extremities; my arms and legs felt numb as I waded across. One by one we made it safely to the other side, and once we were all across we were instructed by the staff to only don one layer of clothing. We scrambled through our kit, all thoughts of being attacked by the enemy were swept from our minds - wet knickers off and all our inhibitions at this point had gone out the window, as eight of the smallest cocks were now on display. We quickly dressed to then be informed that all our kit except our weapons had been lost downriver during the crossing, we were now entering the survival phase of the exercise.

Shit! None of us had been trained in survival. There were no documentary channels or Bear Grylls survival shows on TV back then. We were all clueless, we made our way into a nearby thicket and decided between us what to do. We set about and made a makeshift shelter with branches and bracken and huddled together as night fell, starving and cold.

We lasted one whole night in the woods of Thetford training area, with no real enemy or animals that could kill us, but it served as a vital lesson as to how vulnerable we all were without our personal equipment.

Cadre complete, it was time for our pass off parade. The incentive to do well on the course was that the top three students would get promoted on the parade square - unfortunately I was not one of those 3! For the rest of the candidates who completed the JNCO Cadre were given a period of recommendation. I had been the youngest member on the course, and I was just chuffed to have passed. I was given a recommendation of between 6 to 12 months, meaning a period of time back in my troop to develop and put into practice the leadership skills I had been taught during the course into practice and prove myself worthy of promotion.

I re-joined my squadron, and in the summer of 1990 was deployed to Scotland for one month of prerequisite training in preparation for our up-and-coming construction tour to Kenya. Construction tasks took place in three separate locations. The first was at Barry Budden military range in Dundee, where the support troop, mainly made up of Plant operator mechanics (POMs) and drivers, were tasked with upgrading the existing range roads.

One of the field troops, mainly consisted of Combat Engineers and tradesmen, were accommodated in caravans in a caravan park at the back of a farmyard in Blairgowrie, and aptly named Gypsy Troop, were tasked to build a footbridge, which now spans over the River Ericht by the old oak bank mill.

The rest of us were based at Ballater, a section of Combat Engineers, the QMs department personnel, and the OC, 2i/c and SSM, a small camp normally used by the Guards when Royalty was in residence at Balmoral. The Combat Engineer section was tasked to build a small bridge for the local laird, whose estate lay just north of the town.

I was assigned as the Officer Commanding (OC)'s driver having now completed the JNCO cadre, a job I really didn't want as I would have preferred to be with the lads. But the job had its perks - I got to drive the boss around the Highlands and visited some of the stunning places Scotland had to offer. I also got to do daily runs with the Squadron Sergeant Major (SSM) who had competed in 5 Olympic biathlons over the last 20 years, and I'm sure he got a kick out of thrashing me up and down the Scottish mountains!

Part 5

KENYA

Tension was beginning to build in Iraq as Saddam Hussain prepared to invade Kuwait, but our squadron had already been committed to a six month construction task in Kenya. British forces were now on high alert and preparations were taking place, with our unit becoming a hive of activity. Vehicles were being sprayed desert colour, soldiers were being medically updated and injected with the controversial pyridostigmine bromide as a preventative measure against exposure to chemical agents, now linked to gulf war syndrome. We knew Saddam Hussein used chemical agents on his own people, killing thousands to test its effects, so we were lucky as our squadron had just had several injections in preparation for Kenya, and were therefore exempt from being given the injection with the controversial cocktail of drugs for the time being. However our kit was packed and centrally located within a container, in case we would have to be re-deployed to Iraq.

In early January 1991 we deployed to Kenya under a dark cloud, mocked by the other squadrons as war dodgers. Exercise OAKAPPLE Kenya here we come. Our advance party had flown out prior to Christmas and had been busy setting up the tented camps. Base camp was located next to an airstrip - no buildings, just a large open stretch of land for the odd light aircraft to land. The advance party had constructed around 70 tents including accommodation, medical, cook house, bar, and even a shower tent with a concrete base, which was kitted out with scaffolding to hold the pipe work and with fitted shower heads. The water was gravity fed from a water tank mounted high up on a cuplock tower and was heated by the warm Kenyan sun, providing a nice lukewarm shower.

I was part of the main party and we landed in Nairobi in early January a few days after Christmas leave. As soon as we landed, with no time to stretch our legs, we were immediately directed onto waiting coaches and driven straight up to base camp in Nyeri county. The first two days were spent acclimatising to our surroundings and being briefed on our squadron's overall tasks before being split down and briefed on our own troop task, amongst other things. Each task site was miles apart in different locations.

As part of Support Troop, I was deployed into the Aberdare National Park. There were around 20 of us, a troop sergeant who we named the fat controller, 2 plant fitters, a chef, a dozen plant operators and 2 tipper drivers, myself being one of them. The dusty dirt track took us deep into the National Park to a small clearing with around eight tents -five for sleeping and the others providing a cook's tent, a stores tent and a larger communal tent for eating. In the corner was a large fridge which was to become our honesty bar - one cold beer out was replaced with a warm beer from the stack at the side, and a notepad to write down what we had, which our troop sergeant would monitor and collect the money for from each of us weekly to replenish the stock. The system worked well; a cold beer in the evenings was our solace, a privilege nobody was going to jeopardise by being dishonest.

The camp was relatively small, but ample size for our needs. Three strands of barbed wire separated us from the Kenyan wildlife, and we slept four to a tent on flimsy cot beds which sat around 3 inches off the floor with no ground sheet. There was a small cane mat by the side of our beds that provided a layer in which to stand on whilst you changed, but these soon got infested with termites and they all had to be burned. We had a small metal box about the size of a suitcase that was situated at the end of each cot bed, cleverly hand crafted by a local Kenyan out of old baked bean tins. Our makeshift toilet which was situated away from the tents next to the fence line consisted of a wooden seat with a hole and a bucket underneath, a hessian screen part way around it to offer some privacy. A camp shower was constructed from scaffolding with a 200-litre drum cut in half laid on its side mounted on top, around 7 foot high, with a small tap and an old baked bean tin with several holes was used as a shower head. To the side was another 200-litre drum with its top cut off containing the water, and a small pit was dug underneath the drum for a fire to heat the water.

Showering was a two-man job - whilst one was showering the other was scooping the water with a small bucket from the drum on the floor up into the drum above, a far less luxurious affair than the showers they had at base camp.

Camp maintenance was carried out by two locally employed civilians. Their job was to assist the chef in preparing meals and tend to the camp, ensuring the fire was lit and the water was warm for the evening when we all got back into camp, and generally keeping the area tidy and habitable.

A local ranger was assigned to camp in the evenings, and he would sit by the large open fire we had in the centre of the camp. Armed with his 303 rifles, he would guard the camp from any would-be critters who entered the camp whilst we slept.

The guard would wake the chef early each morning in time for him to prepare breakfast and heat the water ready for us to wash and shave; our troop sergeant would jump on anyone going feral. Reveille every morning was at 05.00 hours. I would grab a stainless-steel wash bowl, scoop out some warm water and wash, shave and clean my teeth prior to breakfast at 05.30, ready to start work at 06:00.

Our troop's task for the next six months was to upgrade over 16 kilometres of roads along the tourist route through the National Park. We dressed in desert boots, green lightweight shorts, with green tee shirt, and carried a machete around our waists, to offer some protection against the wildlife. Tirelessly, we worked 12-hour days with one day off every two weeks - which was a welcome break.

I drove one of the two 15 tonne haulamatic tipper trucks, transporting aggregate from the quarry, along the dirt tracks to the construction team upgrading the roads. The days were long and hot, with no radio, air conditioning or electric windows. Some days the humidity was so high I would wedge the door ajar whilst driving, to create a cool draft. I had the best view anyone could imagine; I would set off for work every morning and watch the sunrise with Mount Kenya as its backdrop, a sight I never got sick of seeing. The wildlife was everywhere: I would see troops of colobus monkeys in the trees, lions hunting warthog, elephants and hyenas, all reminding me of the black and white Tarzan films I used to watch as a child, except that this was in glorious colour.

Once, as I approached a clearing in the trees we referenced as the prairie, 2 female lions lay flat in the wheel ruts which myself and the other driver had created over our time going backwards and forwards. They were using the dry mud ruts as cover to stalk a warthog with its young, some hundred yards away grazing in the open area of grassland. I had no choice but to switch off my engine and watch these magnificent animals hunting. Off to my right was a male lion waiting patiently for his dinner. As the lionesses gave chase, the speed at which the warthog and its young moved was surprising and although I wanted to see a kill I was glad on this occasion that the warthogs outwitted the lionesses.

Elephants are amazing animals and I was lucky enough to have a truly memorable encounter with one once. During monsoon season the old tourist track would turn to mud, work would stop and I would have no choice but to stop my vehicle in the middle of the road and wait it out for an hour or two. With no music to listen to, all I could do was to write a few letters home or catch up on some sleep. I was dosing off with my head against the half open window when I sensed something approaching. I turned my head to see an elephant was standing right alongside my vehicle, his eye was within touching distance and staring right at me. I wound the window down fully, and for a moment was in a stare off with a 7-ton wild animal. He seemed to sense that I was no threat and his stare told me he was just curious and was checking me out - a fleeting moment with nature I will never forget.

I also had the privilege of witnessing a bull elephant in musth (musk) and mating with a female. She was much smaller than the male as he came crashing through the trees into an open area of ground, just a few hundred yards away from where I was servicing my vehicle. His intentions were very clear with his fifth leg swinging from side to side as he charged in pursuit of his prize. I wasn't surprised she was making a run for it, but the poor girl got caught and nature took its course.

My mate was assigned as head banksman at the quarry site. Turnaround time from the quarry to the road construction team varied as time went on, but on average it took me about 45 minutes. One day when I arrived back at the quarry to collect another load on a sweltering hot day he was top off and catching a few rays.

"What the fuck, mate," I said, as the daft sod had covered himself in baby oil thinking he would get a better suntan, and blistered both his shoulders.

He looked like he was sporting a pair of 1980s shoulder pads. Our fat controller sent him to base camp to see the medical officer for treatment and was later charged £50 for causing a self-inflicted injury.

At lunchtime, our troop sergeant would drive round and deliver lunch - a snack and some freshly chopped fruit in Norwegian containers. It was the highlight of the day until around a month into the tour I started to feel unwell. My stomach started to cramp, and I was having to stop every 10 minutes and climb into the back of my tipper with severe diarrhoea. It wasn't a pleasant sight and I was deteriorating quickly so made my way back to camp. The fat controller was not best pleased, he didn't want the job to fall behind and told me to get an hour's sleep and get back to work as the tipper wouldn't drive itself. Luckily for me the medical officer was carrying out a site visit and took one look at me and drove me straight back to base camp. I was now in a bad condition. He gave me a litre of dioralyte to replace the salts in my body I had lost through diarrhoea, but I couldn't keep it down and it was now coming out of both ends at the same time. He immediately administered a drip into my arm and by next morning I was admitted to the local hospital in Mweiga.

The nurse on the ward looking after me, passed me a large tablet on a small tray. I looked up at her and told her I couldn't swallow it; she smiled and took advantage of my now weakened state and rolled me over to one side and shoved it in my butt - not a pleasant moment for either of us.

I was diagnosed with dysentery, an infection in my intestine, and by the following morning after being violated by the nurse every four hours with a large pill and a fat finger, I was greeted by several other members of my troop - not a visit as I first thought, but they also had similar symptoms and were admitted onto the same ward. They were all diagnosed with gastroenteritis, a bacterial tummy bug and given medicine orally, and found great amusement by my four hourly visits from the nurse.

It was later found to be one of the locally employed camp maintenance men - he was emptying the shit bucket as part of his daily chores without the use of disposable gloves. He was then assisting the chef in preparing the fruit which was being delivered to us at lunchtimes. It was later joked that I must have eaten a piece of the fat controller's shit, and that's why I had the worst illness!

I was discharged from hospital three days later and two stone lighter and driven back to base camp, where I was ordered to report to the OC. I was thinking he was concerned about my wellbeing but I was even more surprised to hear that my promotion had come through and he awarded me my first stripe; I was now Lance Corporal Roberts.

On a day off we would travel back down to base camp, with my first port of call being a luxury shower with a concrete floor instead of the half broken pallet we used to keep our feet from getting muddy, before heading off to our favourite spot, the Aberdare Country Club for a few beers and a round of golf. My golfing skills were pretty crap, but it was fun watching the local baboons stealing our golf balls off the fairway and chasing after them swinging a 5 iron.

I was now four months in and it was time for some much-needed rest and recuperation (R&R). For seventy quid I went on the R&R package which the SSM had arranged and travelled to Watamu on the east coast next to the Indian Ocean. We set off by coach to Nairobi before catching the overnight sleeper train to Mombasa. A bottle of cheap whiskey and a deck of cards always helped to break up the boredom, and after the usual shenanigans, singing and doing the conga, we eventually arrived in Mombasa early the next morning. We had a few hours to wait before catching the coach to Watamu, so we elected to go to the zoo to kill a bit of time. Living in the national park for the last four months surrounded by wildlife and we chose to go to the zoo! It was purely because there were no bars close by, which was probably best as I'm sure that otherwise we would have missed our connection.

Happy Nights chalets, situated at the top end of the small town of Watamu was to be our accommodation for the next week or so; nothing fancy but it was clean with a proper bed. Bags dropped, we wasted no time and soon made our way through the small town and down to the beach - pure white sand and crystal-clear ocean was like a scene from a James Bond film, a far cry from Rhyl beach.

Exploring the coastline, we came across three plush hotels, Turtle Bay Beach Resort, Hemingway's, and Ocean Sports which had one of those wooden frames used to hang big fish from on the beach.

The local girls were on to us the first night and my roommate started sleeping with a local girl called November. She was around 6 foot tall with long braided hair and we rather cruelly nicknamed her 'the Predator', as her features closely resembled the alien creature in the classic film starring Arnold Schwarzenegger.

He woke up one morning complaining of a sore throat. I took one look at him and "Jesus' his neck was visibly swollen, and he was finding it very difficult to swallow.

I knew the medical officer (MO) had flown his wife over and they were staying in one of the plush hotels on the oceanfront, so I said,

"Come on, let's go and see what he thinks".

As we walked the beach towards the hotel, luck had it that they were both sitting eating breakfast on the terrace at the front of their hotel. Not knowing at the time that his wife was also a doctor, I said,

"Sorry to bother you, Doc," and I went on to explain about my mate's throat, as he was now hardly able to speak for himself. They both took one look at him, looked at each other and said "gonorrhoea". He had broken the cardinal rule when having sex with a local and paid the price.

We spent the days like most tourists on holiday, snorkelling in the sea and lounging around. The Sports Bar and Hemingway's were our favourite watering holes, and the staff were friendly and made us feel welcome even though we weren't residents of the hotels.

We soon found ourselves disembarking the train back in Nairobi after a relatively quiet down-beat overnight train journey, We had an extra night so we booked a cheap hotel room and decided to go and eat later that evening in "Carnivores", a fabulous and famous restaurant which served up all of Kenya's wildlife from zebra to crocodile.

Back to work and the days started to drag after our break to the coast; I was now in a different state of mind, and looking forward to my day off as well as counting the days before I get to sleep in a proper bed.

Whilst sitting at our usual table on the veranda of the country club, four of us decided to go around the country park on horseback - it was a spur of the moment idea. There was a notice in the club advertising it, so for a laugh we decided to give it a go. The tour guide gave us a quick brief and asked if any of us had ridden a horse before. We assured him this was our first time as he passed us a helmet each and we walked up towards the stables. The names on the stable doors read, Lightning, Thunderbolt, and 2 other equally terrifying names and our joviality soon turned into dreaded fear. I was allocated Lightning, and as I hesitantly donned the helmet the thoughts of 'I'm not coming back alive' ran through my head as we all glanced across at each other thinking, 'is it not too late to call this off?'.

None of us were wanting to chicken out as we saddled up and set off. I was anticipating a Grand National start and I began to plan how this was going to go - do I wrap my arms around the beast's neck and hold on for dear life, or do I leap off and take the hit? My fears soon diminished when old Lightning decided he wasn't going anywhere, he just stood there motionless.

"Well come on, do something," talking to him as if he knew what the heck I was saying. Nope - nothing! He just stood there. The tour guide shouted across to kick back gently which I did. Jesus! He bolted - well more of a sudden movement - but it was enough for me to almost shit myself.

As we casually strolled around the Kenyan bush, thoughts of being stalked and attacked by a lion came to mind. We were only a few miles from the National Park, what if one escaped and leapt out of the bush and attacked us? Would lightning rear up, throwing me to the ground and leg it? 'Shut up Kev', I thought, just enjoy the moment.

Our time in Kenya was now coming to an end. All our construction tasks had been completed. It was time to strip out the satellite camps and move back to base camp. The job of cleaning and returning all stores, tents, and equipment back to the British Army Training Unit Kenya (BATUK) based in Nairobi began. Without hesitation I volunteered to stay behind when the bulk of the squadron flew back to the UK. I stayed for a further 2 weeks with around 15 other guys to make up the rear party under the direction of the Quartermaster (QM).

Nairobi being around a two-hour drive away, the gonorrhoea king and I, along with our co-passengers were tasked to drive the stores trucks - two trips a day over the next four days we anticipated to backload all of the resources and equipment.

We both set off on the first day and as we crossed over a bridge near the capital, a young boy was eagerly waving a fish half his size in the hope that someone would stop and buy it. As each day passed the young boy was still waving the fish desperately hoping someone would stop, and as the days passed the fish seemed to have less movement and became a bit stiffer, but the boy kept smiling and waving his arms eager for us to stop. We were on a tight deadline and the deadly potholed roads made the journey slower and not wanting to be on the roads at night due to the dangers of other road users, we decided to bag up some goodies for the young lad as he kept us entertained during the tedious journey back and forth - it was the least we could do to give him something for his efforts. The last few trips we would slowdown and toss him a small bag of sweets and biscuits, he would fling the fish on the floor and hold his hands out waiting for his next cache of goodies. I guess we were as excited to give it to him as he was to receive it!

With Base camp now packed up and loaded up with the last remaining tents we headed to Nairobi one last time. The days were spent cleaning the stores and returning them to the stores, and we would spend the evenings exploring the bars and clubs of Nairobi. We stuck to the main hotspots in the city; the "Casino", "Buffalo Bill's" and "Florida 2000" were the usual haunts we would visit. One night 6 of us piled into one taxi and headed from the casino at the top of the hill to "Flo's". As the taxi driver headed down the hill he started pumping his brakes yelling, "No brakes," as he tried to time his run towards the traffic lights ahead. Luckily for us he went through on green and coasted the car along until he was slow enough to bump into the kerb. The taxi fare was only a few shillings and he was delighted when we gave him enough cash to get his brakes fixed.

We returned to Waterbeach in the summer of 1991 and the other squadrons having recovered from their time in the desert during Op Granby, the regiment organised an all ranks party within our support troop hanger. A large stage was erected and we were entertained by the 1970s rock'n'roll band Showaddywaddy, a group I grew up listening to, and to watch them perform in our hanger with their colourful Teddy boy suits was pretty surreal.

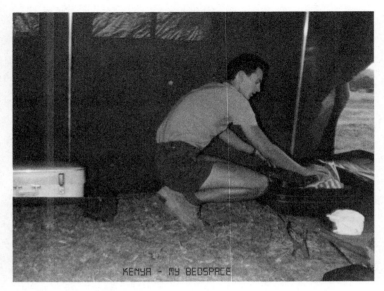

KENYA - MY BEDSPACE

KENYA - ELEPHANT

KENYA - EXERCISE BAR & CAMP TOILET

KENYA - SHOWER

KENYA - READING LETTER (BLUEY)

KENYA - HORSE NAMED LIGHTNING

WATAMU (INDIAN OCEAN) R&R

KENYA - LION PRIDE (NOTE THE EYE SHINE)

Part 6

CANADA 1992

A tradition at Christmas is for the corporals to invite the warrant officers and sergeants over to the Corporals' Mess for Christmas drinks. It would normally start around lunchtime and still in uniform, the drinking usually carried on well into the evening and often ended in carnage. We were all well-oiled when our sergeant major decided to leave. One of my fellow lance corporals decided it would be a good idea to hold his drill stick hostage in return for a round of drinks.

"OK, where's my stick?" he asked and was met with, "Not until you've bought a round, sir".

Obligingly, he bought a round, which was followed by a loud cheer from several of the recipients. However, the next morning at 07:00 was our pre-Christmas shutdown room inspection. As the sergeant major was doing his rounds he grinned at me and told me to get outside and report to a staff sergeant who was waiting with all the other JNCO's who had been involved in the hostage crisis the previous night. Lined up, he marched us in single file towards the direction of the guardroom, a good 400 yards away from the accommodation block, but instead of turning us right in the direction of the guardroom, he steered us left towards a lone soldier holding open a door to an empty shipping container. We marched in and the door was slammed shut behind us.

Seven already blurry eyed junior corporals were now in total darkness and stumbling around and smelling like a brewery, and wondering what the heck had just happened. It wasn't long before the chuntering began, and we were all thinking, 'we won't be going on our 2 weeks of Christmas leave in a few hours' time'.

An hour passed. We soon began to hear voices and movement outside. We heard the distinctive clatter as the shipping container handles opened and the doors were flung open. Not knowing what to expect we were greeted by the sergeant major holding his stick aloft in one hand with a smirk on his face, and two soldiers on his flank, poised ready, holding a fire hose now pointed firmly in our direction,

"Let 'em have it," he yelled as a jet of water unleashed towards us.

After a good soaking and dripping wet he marched us in double time back to the squadron offices and paraded us in front of the rest of the squadron who were waiting eagerly to be dismissed for Christmas break, but not before the sergeant major had the last laugh.

"The morale of the story," he said, "don't ever fuck with the sergeant major," and in all fairness he played a blinder.

A few months later I arrived in Canada. A small attachment of around 30 or so, we were split down into support sections, a section to be embedded in support of each company and a section to act as the Batsims (Battlefield Simulation) for the 1st Battalion, The Royal Highland Fusiliers. I was placed in the Batsims section as second in command for the six-week duration.

The exercise took place on the vast training area of Wainwright, in the state of Alberta. My role was to prepare the explosive charges and place them down range to create an effective battlefield scene for the battlegroup as the men moved around the area, under controlled live firing conditions. The explosives would give a sense of realism to the exercise and create a spectacular battlefield scene.

Due to the restrictions imposed in Britain to what live firing training can be carried out, Canada provides one of the best training grounds for larger scale live firing in which British soldiers can train.

We were tasked prior to the sections being embedded with the battlegroup, to build a footbridge across a small river, known as NEB (None Equipment Bridging). Using trees from a nearby wood to provide us with the materials needed, we set about cutting and stripping trees and doing what Royal Engineers do best, and 24hrs later a fully functional footbridge was erected. The other engineer sections were now embedded with their companies and the battlegroup crossed the bridge marking the beginning of the exercise. Our first BATSIM task came through - we were ordered to carry out a controlled bridge demolition. We drove a Land Rover across to test its strength, we estimated it to be at least a class 5t - not bad considering the speed and materials used - it was a shame we went and blew it to bits!

One of the guys in my section was a keen canoeist, and he had recently passed his canoeing instructors' course just prior to arriving in Canada. The adventure training team was being sent to Jasper, in the Rocky Mountains, to set up a 5 day adventure training package, which everyone would be given time off to participate in at some point during the 6 weeks. However, they were short of canoeing instructors and they somehow got wind that we had a qualified instructor with us. They asked if he could be released to support the adventure training team. Of course he left kicking and screaming and I was now one man short.

Somewhat bewildered, a pioneer sergeant was soon allocated to us as a replacement, a big fella and sporting a long thick beard with hardly a tooth left in his head. The beard is a pioneers' tradition dating back to the 1700s and he was as mad as a hatter. Curious as to why we had been allocated a sergeant as a replacement, he was happy to explain about his pending court martial. And the reason why I asked?

"I accidentally on purpose shot one of my own men," he said. That was an opening statement if ever I've heard one! He went on to explain about his party trick.

"To put the fear of God into one of my fresh-faced soldiers. I would remove the bullet head off a 7.62 mm live round, empty the powder and then replace the bullet head, unbeknown to the soldier of course. I would load the round into the chamber of my SLR which was the issued weapon at the time, and pull the trigger."

At this point he further explained how the bullethead would just drop out the end of the barrel, something he assured us he had done many times before.

The British Army around this time was phasing out the 7.62mm SLR and replacing it with the modern 5.56mm small arms SA80. Everyone knew the weapon did not pack a punch anywhere near that of the SLR because of the smaller calibre bullet, but that was the whole point of issuing a less lethal weapon - the idea being if you shot the enemy with a more powerful weapon 9 times out of 10 he would die instantly on the battlefield, so the reasoning behind the change, apart from other attributes, was it created more casualties. Sounds crazy but the more casualties the more impact it has on the enemy, psychologically when men are screaming, but also so the enemy won't advance as they will be busy recovering their wounded. He further went on to explain,

"So I never considered a practice run, and I ended up putting a hole through the young lad's shoulder". Wow! And now you're here with us playing with explosives. We set about rigging up an explosive ring main, laying out hundreds of metres of black and tan wire in a large loop, from our firing position and down range over 300m and back. Each of us took bets on who could make the most impressive explosion, I opted to strap some plastic bottles of petrol and diesel to my charge and placed it in the turret of an old rusted battle tank; the tank had been given a good hammering over the years and I was hoping to finally demolish it.

We cleared the range to allow for our Troopy (a young 2nd lieutenant often referred to as Troopy instead of sir as a less informal way of address an officer when operating out in the field) and our section commander to attach the fuses we had placed to the ring main; the range was now live. With the range ready all that was left to do was to wait for nightfall and the arrival of the fusiliers to take up their defensive positions in the trenches in front of our firing position. A message came over the radio, informing us the brigadier was flying in to watch the evening's exercise, so we laid out a luminous helicopter landing marker behind our firing position in readiness for him.

As the light began to fade, we could hear the distinctive noise of an approaching Gazelle helicopter as it drew closer and landed behind us. Troopy's nerves showed as he was fiddling with the shrike, pressing the continuity several times, reassuring himself everything was ready to go, before running over to greet the big man.

The pioneer sergeant, forever the prankster, decided to play a practical joke and removed the livewire from the shrike and replaced it with a short length of trailing wire, placing it back as Troopy had left it. Troopy arrived back with the Brigadier now in tow; we were now in full darkness as he briefed the boss quietly. We could just about hear the exercising troops moving Into position just below us.

"To our front, sir, is our infantry platoon, now in the trenches in a defensive position. Down range we have set up explosive charges waiting for you to do the honours and light up the range by pressing these buttons. When you're ready, sir, light up the range."

The blood drained from the young commander's face as the one-star general pressed the firing button, and fuck all happened as the young troop commander's short lived career flashed before his eyes. But to be fair, the brigadier was the first to laugh. Schoolboy chuckles over, and with no harm done, the pioneer sergeant owned up and handed him the end of the live wires and it was back to business, button eventually pressed and like a conductor, the huge explosions went off one by one, boom...boom....boom, no second guesses for who won the bet for the most dramatic explosion, but more impressive was the quick reaction as the fusiliers' machine gun fire and tracer lit up the sky seconds later, section commanders' screaming fire control orders as the smell of cordite filled the air. You could feel the awesome firepower, like thunder, thumping you in the chest, Gympies (GPMGs) began to glow in the dark as thousands of rounds heated up their barrels, Shamooli flares lit up the night sky, and with large explosions still ringing in my ears the firing suddenly stopped. The infantry soldiers unloaded their weapons and made safe and bugged out, The silence was literally deafening - a magnificent show of firepower and dominance that was truly impressive.

Time to pack up and hit the town, and allow for Troopy to unwind and return back to earth after his near career ending moment with the brigadier.

The town of Wainwright is bustling with restaurants and bars, some of which have live bands. At the time Nirvana seemed to be the only group they knew as they continued to play it in every bar we ventured into.

The odd titi bar gave a nice reprieve from listening to the same tunes over and over and was only a short taxi ride away. The access road skirted around the camp's perimeter fence, and you could see the town's lights across a large open field opposite the guardroom. The field is home to a large male buffalo, and a commemorative plaque next to the gate stood as a stark reminder to any would-be alcohol fuelled soldiers wanting to take the short cut into town. A young marine was tragically killed a year earlier when he decided to take his chance, and now a warning sign in bold letters on the gate states - unless you can run over 40mph, it is strongly recommended you get a taxi!.

After a night of swilling pitchers of beer and with Nirvana still pounding in my head, the rest of the day making large explosions made for a long hangover. Keen to see the day over we made our way back into camp for tea, parked our vehicles on the vehicle park and went over to the cookhouse. Whilst walking past the helipad I felt the urge to throw caution to the wind and enquire about a spin in one of the helicopters. There were two Gazelle helicopters sitting on the pan and I always wondered what it would be like to take a ride; strange when all day all I was eager to do was get back to the room and hit the pillow. The rest of the lads headed on to the cookhouse, and one shouted,

"Don't waste your time, they'll only tell you to fuck off". But with my mind set I walked down the short hill to the cabin beside the helipad, knocked on the door and entered. A flight sergeant was sitting there behind his desk, and after a brief intro, I came straight out with it and asked him,

"Any chance of going for a spin in a helicopter?"

The guy looked at me in disbelief and after getting over my none too subtle question said,

"Yeah, no problem. You're in luck. I'm taking one up on a test flight after dinner. Come back at 6 and there's room for two more".

The guy was sound, and momentarily I had forgotten about my hangover which had plagued me all day. I made my way up the hill to the cookhouse to join the lads. Feeling smug, I waited for an opening.

"So, waste of time then, Kev?"

Containing my excitement, I calmly replied,

"Not really. Who fancies a spin in a helicopter?"

"Fuck off, you're having us on".

Three of us arrived at the helipad, my companions still a bit hesitant, wondering whether or not I was pulling their legs. It was a hot summer's evening and not a cloud in sight. The pilot gave us a few safety points, we hopped on board and strapped in, and then we lifted off. He took the helicopter straight up and hovered around 2000 feet; slowly rotating the helicopter 360 degrees the pilot pointed out prominent landmarks of interest: Calgary, 250 miles to our west towards the Rocky mountains, Edmonton 130 miles north west ,with Saskatchewan province only 30 miles to our east. I had the perfect view, but as I felt myself yawning I jokingly said over the radio,

"Any chance we can fly a bit of TAC (Tactical), Captain?" thinking at that moment I was in a Vietnam movie. He glanced across at me and smirked, flicking the joystick to one side and we dropped out of the sky and into a steep dive.

"Holy shiiiit!" as I reached for the invisible passenger brake pedal wishing I'd kept my big mouth shut. We dropped out of the sky like a lead balloon and the longest rollercoaster ride began. As we approached earth and feeling like we were about to plunge into the river, he levelled off, trees now flew past either side of us and it felt like we were skimming just above the water; Battle River is so called as it runs through the training area. With trees now a bit too close for my liking we sped along the contours of the river like a Formula One racing car. My heart was pounding with excitement as I fought to keep my dinner down! We quickly approached a sharp bend in the river. I felt myself tense up as if bracing for impact and still subconsciously reaching for the imaginary brake pedal, but he pulled back on the joystick and out we popped up above the treeline. I bet he thought, 'that'll shut the cocky git up'.... he thought right!

Back on earth, it was time for our section to head to Jasper for some adventure training. We opted to travel in the back of the baggage wagon instead of by coach with the infantry guys - nothing against them but we had a few crates of beer to swill and knew the coach driver would not allow alcohol onboard. Our only problem was the lack of toilet facilities - drinking all that beer, it needs to come out at some point. The small holes in the floor of the back of the military troop carrying vehicle was our only option. The vehicles who followed must have wondered whether our vehicle had a coolant leak as they used their windscreen wipers during that hot summer's day.

After several hours on the road we eventually arrived at the gateway to the Rockies, and last chance to grab a big Mac and chips before heading into the wilderness.

I couldn't believe what I was seeing when we pulled in, not just the stunning and outstanding picturesque view of the Rocky Mountain range for the first time, but also the queues of coaches lined up outside McDonald's, people going mad for their last chance to grab some fast food before entering the national park.

Day one, a 30 Km mountain bike ride along the ridges high up above Jasper awaited us. Bikes loaded up in the back of the 4 tonner to transport us up to the drop off point high up in the mountains, we were met by the local park ranger who briefed us, warning us of the local wildlife, and to be on the lookout for bears.

"Yes gentlemen, you are in bear country."

We set off, slightly dubious about how we would tackle a bear if he happened to be sightseeing on the same route. Nevertheless, the scenery was stunning! The Columbia Mountain, the highest peak in Alberta at an elevation of 3782 metres, acted as a backdrop to the town of Jasper thousands of feet below, with the Athabasca River flowing along its flank making for an incredible sight. And not a glimpse of a bear to be seen which left me slightly relieved, but also a little bit disappointed.

As the day drew to a close we arrived back at the tented camp and time for a quick half hour's nap before dinner. A commotion around camp grabbed my attention, and peering through the tent door from the comfort of my camp bed, guys were walking past, cameras in hand. A black bear had entered our campsite, no doubt attracted by the smell of food. We were briefed to remain in our tents with the tent flaps buttoned closed in such an event, so it's funny how our first reaction was to ignore any orders which would endanger life and instead, reach for our cameras. Around 30 of us were now gathered outside our tents, cameras busy clicking away. I guess feeling outnumbered he casually made his way back into the woods, but we sure as hell made certain the tent flaps were shut tight that night!

Day 2, Athabasca glacier is one of the six principal toes of the British Columbia icefield, and the source of the Athabasca River. It's a sheet of ice around 10,000 years old and a place where you can see the effects of global warming. Its huge marker posts show how it has receded 1.5 kilometres in the last 125 years. Deciding not to take the specially modified tourist buses mounted on huge tracks, which ferried the tourists up onto the ice sheet, the 4 of us decided to hike our way up. Probably not the best decision - the huge frozen glacier which seemed a small challenge was now much more intimidating up close and personal, than from the view back at the car park when we first arrived. As we looked back the car park could now only be made out by the colours of the coaches. The cracks in the ice now became crevasses as we held each other's arms, peeking over the edge for a glimpse, and that is where my faithful camera now bloody lies, hundreds of feet below!

Day 3, White water rafting was next on the agenda. Another challenging experience, our Canadian oarsman was more than excited to have a group of fit military men on board. Instead of the usual mismatched individuals from all walks of life grouped together, he finally got a group he knew could respond quickly to orders and he couldn't wait to get us on the water. We agreed for him to take us down the hardest and most dangerous route of the river; he couldn't contain his excitement as he briefed us on the do's and don'ts of white water rafting. As he explained, he never gets to ride the rapids aggressively; he had to be extra cautious with civilian passengers in the boat. He explained that he needed to be in full control of the raft at all times. And his final words before we entered the rapids were

"It's important you do not enter my space at the back of the raft".

We set off from the bank in relatively calm water. You could see the river ahead was looking pretty choppy and within minutes we entered the rapids. He was steering the raft into the rough parts of the river, and we were being tossed about like rag dolls in a washing machine. He was shouting orders like "hard on the left," for the guys sitting on the left side of the boat to start paddling their oars as hard and as fast as they could and in sync with one another to steer away from any danger, and then shouting, "all together," so we moved in a forward direction. We were nailing it and the instructor was shouting with joy,

"Yeah man, this is great guys, you're doing brilliant". And then the front of the boat hit a rock square on, the concertina effect ejected the instructor from the back of the raft towards the front - a good 10 feet. I looked down at him and said,

"Not so fucking joyful now are you!".

Our final day was a more leisurely affair, canoeing around one of the mountain lakes with our keen canoeist who had deserted us weeks earlier. He was grinning from ear to ear like a Cheshire cat having spent the last 4 weeks swanning it in Jasper.

As luck would have it, my section and I were given the opportunity to spend a further 4 days in Edmonton on our way back from the Rockies. We obviously jumped at the chance and took great delight in telling our deserter to keep on paddling! The look on his face was peach. I don't suppose he was really bothered that much, but it made us feel good.

Our time there was mostly spent in the famous West Edmonton Mall, the largest mall in North America. Jurassic Park was being premiered in the cinema a month prior to its release in the UK and the must-see film of its time. We opted for the afternoon viewing and sitting in the front row of the cinema eating popcorn was a surreal experience, but well worth the bragging rights to family back home!

Later, we stumbled across a pub with a distinctive Scottish sound bellowing into the night air. Inside we found a load of guys from the fusiliers with their ugliest member sitting in the corner squeezing the life out of a set of bagpipes, a clever lad using his musical talent to attract the women, and to be fair he was entertaining - nothing beats the sound of the pipes.

Time to leave the beautiful state of Alberta and return to the UK. And back into the swing of mundane life in barracks, Monday morning parades, PT parades and a not so favourite of mine - vehicle maintenance. Welcome news was soon announced by the OC during the squadron parade one Monday morning and it brought a smile to my face. We were off to Canada again on a 6-month construction tour. We were later briefed in more detail and informed we would be based at Base Borden in the state of Ontario, a military camp about an hour's drive north of Toronto. For the married personnel this came as bad news as they didn't want to leave their families, or be at the end of the grief they knew they would get from their wives, something I didn't need to worry about at this stage in my life.

I immediately volunteered to fly out with the advance party two weeks before the main body. Little did I know at the time of volunteering that the advance party was to fly by C130 Hercules transporter plane, loaded with our squadron's construction tools and excess baggage.

Propeller planes, unless carrying enough fuel to cross the Atlantic, need to fly overland where possible, another little something I hadn't previously known in my haste to volunteer. It meant our journey would take 2 days and our flight path took us from Brize Norton in Oxfordshire, north over Scotland and across into Reykjavik in Iceland where we were to refuel with an overnight stop. In Reykjavik we were ordered to remain in the hotel for the night, and handed 30 US dollars for food and a drink. But of course, we did just the opposite, and left the hotel through the rear kitchen door so as not to be caught by our seniors. After a night on the town dressed in military uniform and attracting some attention from the native females, sadly we contained ourselves and snuck back into the hotel the same way we escaped a few hours earlier. The next morning, we set off over Greenland and eventually landed in Toronto, at Pearson International Airport.

Our tented camp was situated around 3 kilometres into the training area of the main camp of Borden, a pretty good setup to be fair, with no real complaints about the camp's facilities. The shower blocks were portable temporary cabins with hot running water, and we had a large tented bar with a TV area and satellite TV. The only complaint we had at the time was we arrived during black fly hatching season. Having just endured 2 days cramped up in a noisy prop plane with bits of cargo sticking in every rib, I was now being eaten alive. A black swarm and a low buzzing noise filled the air which made daily tasks over the following few weeks extremely irritating. We were tasked to knock 6ft steel pickets into the ground to mark out the boundary for the vehicle park. We set about using a post pounder, a heavy hollow tool weighted at the top end, it slides over the top of the fence post like a sleeve with handles either side. Ideally used by 2 people you raise it up and pound it down onto the fence picket, driving the picket into the ground. It can also be used by one person holding both handles but that's hard graft when wearing a head net and gloves and plagued by flies.

I was attached to the main project for the duration of the tour, the construction of a battle tank bridge across the Borden River, that runs from Borden Lake in the north to James Bay basin in the south and passes directly through the training area. Bridging this obstacle would allow direct access from one side of the training area to the other without the need for the exercising vehicles entering the main base.

The other squadron task was the building of a kitchen facility and canteen, which also stopped exercising troops from having to head back to the main base during mealtimes, reducing the impact on training.

Construction began with felling trees through the forest to allow for access and egress to the bridge site as the plague of black fly and mosquitos began to subside. The plant hire equipment began to arrive, and I was finally given the keys to a brand new 20t Terex Frame Steer Dump Truck, a vehicle I had never driven before, an awesome piece of kit but it felt weird to drive at first as the vehicle turns from the centre behind the driving position and took some getting used to.

As with any construction work, trying to keep ahead of deadlines is key. The days were long and progress was good, but we needed to factor in some extra shifts or longer hours to keep ahead of schedule to allow for any setbacks or colossal fuck ups. Just like when our excavator operator got his vehicle bogged in so deep, it was unable to self-recover. The mud and water was 2 feet above the tracks and the suction it created was too powerful for the excavator to extend its arm and drag itself out. This was a big embarrassment for the OC, as he had to go cap in hand to ask the Canadian military for assistance. A few hours later a leopard recovery tank arrived to drag the heavily bogged down excavator out of its mud pit; the tank crew were not impressed as their recovery tank had just been re-painted and polished in preparation for an upcoming show.

Driving my Terex back to site one morning I encountered a skunk on the dirt track up ahead. I decided it would be funny to give chase, as it ran along the track in front of me. Not intending to hurt the animal I kept enough space between us to avoid running him over, but I soon realised this was not a clever move. His tail went up and he let rip. I knew skunks give off a bad smell - I grew up watching the cartoon, Pepe le Pew - but I never anticipated how bad the smell was going to be. I was 10 feet up in my cab, the door in the open locked position so the smell wafted straight into the cab when the smell hit me. Slamming on the anchors I stopped immediately, jumping out of my seat, I stood on the platform bent over the safety rail physically retching, as the dirty little bastard ran off having had the last laugh.

Days off, and depending on the weather we would drive up to Wasaga beach, the longest freshwater beach in the world. Once there we would chill out, playing a bit of beach football or volleyball with a few cold beers from the nearby liquor store.

The CN Tower in Toronto was another favourite of mine. Experiencing the glass door lift as it set off from the ground was quite something! It took 58 seconds to reach the main deck, and everyone in the lift would soon step back away from the door as the lift went up. After a few beers and a bite to eat in the revolving restaurant, we would go up in another lift to the space pod, one of the highest observation platforms in the world. At 1465 ft high, you can feel the tower swaying on a windy day and I could see the mist off Niagara Falls a hundred 100 miles away. The Skylon tower at Niagara is tiny compared to the CN Tower but allows you to view the awesome power of the falls from high above.

Our time in Canada was coming to an end and the profits made from the squadron bar were put towards an entertainment night. The sergeant major hired a hypnotist for the evening, preparations had been made, a large wooden stage was constructed between the bar tent and the woodland to the rear, well stocked with beer and spirits and a large buffet had been laid out. The evening was warm and dry and things were going with a swing.

It was time for the hypnotist to start his show; he addressed the squadron and asked if we would like the show to be tame or wild. Of course we all shouted wild, and he asked for 12 volunteers to join him onstage. He sat them down on plastic chairs in a half circle facing the squadron and put them to sleep. The odd two or three who didn't go under were kindly asked to leave the stage, and then he started off getting those left to do silly things, from hopping around the stage like frogs to barking loudly at the moon - that sort of stuff. Once he was happy he had control of them he asked for 10 more volunteers to join him on stage of whom I was one. He put his hypnotised guests back to sleep and asked us to start dancing on the stage. The audience was already laughing at our shit dancing, but then he told his subjects that when he clicked his fingers they would see dancing before them ten of the most beautiful women in the world.

"One...two...three...click."

The guys woke up and started rubbing their thighs in excitement before getting up off their chairs and making advances towards us. I was already feeling a little bit awkward about being eyed up by one of the lads, but then he made his move grabbing my tits and telling me he loved me – it was definitely the weirdest thing that ever happened to me, but we played the part and thank god after a few minutes the hypnotist put an end to it. He told them that when the music changed these beautiful women before them would become the ugliest women in the world. The look on their faces was priceless, and the guy soon let go of my tits. The hypnotist then put them back to sleep on the plastic chairs and we left the stage.

He then informed his subjects that when they woke up they were to demonstrate how they would have a sexy time with the beautiful women they danced with earlier using the plastic chairs. "One...two...three...click." Carnage ensued on the stage, there was chair slapping going on and lots of "yee-haws" being shouted as the guys showed off their bedroom antics, but top marks went to one lad who had everyone doubled over as he ran off into the trees and all you could see was his arse bobbing in and out. What a way to end a six month tour!

CANADA - IMPROVISED
BOMB MAKING

CANADA - IMPROVISED BOMB EXPLODING

CANADA - HELI PAD

CANADA - FLY
TACT CAPTAIN

CANADA - START OF TASK

CANADA - MY FSDT BEING LOADED

CANADA - MID TASK

CANADA - TASK CLOSE TO FINISH

Part 7

NORTHERN IRELAND 93/95

I was promoted to full corporal and sent on a 2-year posting to Northern Ireland as part of Operation Banner. The name given to the British Armed Forces deployment to the province during the troubles, which lasted 38 years, from August 1969 until its dissolution in July 2007, making it the British Army's longest continuous deployment.

I boarded the plane at Manchester and after a short 50 minute flight I landed at Belfast City Airport, now known as George Best Airport. The experience of travelling to Northern Ireland alone for the first time was pretty daunting. The horror stories and reports we had all heard on the news added to my fear. When I landed I reported to the Smith Airways desk (an airline desk acting as a cover for all military personnel arriving at the airport) - the powers that be who came up with that name must have been geniuses - Smith Airways....really! However the alternative of jumping in the wrong taxi and asking to be taken to a military base could have had serious consequences.

At the back of Smith Airways, I waited for the duty driver to take myself and others off the flight safely to Massereene Barracks in Antrim. The camp's new accommodation blocks were in the process of being built, so for now I was accommodated in Tenko, fittingly named after the 70's TV drama about British prisoners of war living in shacks in Japanese prison camps during WW11.

Excited to begin, I spent the rest of the evening trying to sew my new stripes on the arm of my shirt, ready to report to the sergeant major the following morning. My excitement was soon shattered when he assigned me as the regimental fuels and transport corporal, my dream of commanding my own section put on hold for now. Instead I was in charge of oil drums, lubricants, fuel and the civilian petrol pump attendant. I could hardly contain my excitement!

I decided to up the ante and for £30 a year I joined the regimental golf society; having never hit a golf ball in my life I could now escape the mundane choir of fuel accounting and have access to some of Northern Ireland's top golf courses. I was utterly useless, but the courses were spectacular.

A few weeks in and I attended my Northern Ireland Reinforcement Training (NIRTT) in Ballykinler, A mandatory course to highlight the current threat level and current tactics being used by the paramilitaries. Once complete you were also authorised to carry a 9mm pistol when on official duty within the province. The course also highlighted the danger zones better known as Red, Amber or White areas; the white areas were normally open areas away from towns and villages or main transit routes through the city, while the amber and red areas are hotspots where terrorists have been known to be operating. Each morning we would have briefings on the current threat levels, and any activities which may have occurred over the last 24hrs. There was always a shooting, a sectarian killing or a bombing which would have occurred and unless it had a huge impact, it was never televised or broadcast on mainland UK TV.

On the pistol range I practised drawing my pistol and cocking it, ensuring I had the correct grip on the weapon. It takes time to put all the motions together; the idea is not to go to too fast like you're some kind of Billy the Kid, but slower and smoother is the key. Most of the day on the range was spent engaging the targets from the standing position, and as confidence grew, we progressed to sitting in a plastic chair facing the target as though in a vehicle and pointed the weapon slightly away and to the right away from my body, simulating firing through the open driver's side window, then turning the chair to the left as if to shoot out of the driving position to the side, and vice versa.

Forward rolls followed, with side rolls off the chair, drawing the pistol and engaging the target with two to three live rounds, all the time keeping 100% focused. It would be very easy and extremely painful to get over excited and shoot yourself in the bollocks. It brought back memories of my childhood, running around the woods with a stick and rolling around, except this was serious and definitely not child's play. Tumbling around and drawing a live pistol is a very dangerous manoeuvre, which accentuated the need for this type of drill.

The next day we headed down to the loop, an area about the size of a premiership football pitch, with steep banks all round and a tarmac road you can drive a car around. Electronic targets lay hidden in the undergrowth and would pop up when activated by the Directing Staff (DS). Buddying up, we took turns driving. We set off around the circuit around 25mph, my heart beating like a drum, anticipating when and where the targets would pop up. A group of targets soon popped up to our front, and I screamed,

"Ambush, targets front!" and ordered a passenger side exit from the vehicle, "Debus, passenger side", as I slammed on the anchors bringing the vehicle to a dead stop and at a slight angle to offer more protection on the passenger side. I drew my pistol, placing the rear sight against the base of the steering wheel and forcing the handgrip forward, cocked it one-handed which allowed me to keep control of the steering wheel with my left hand. I pointed my pistol out the window towards the targets and fired off a couple of rounds, giving my buddy time to exit the vehicle and take up a solid firing position, kneeling in the crease of the open door and providing covering fire.

He shouted, "Move!" my cue to exit the vehicle. I scrambled over the passenger seat and with adrenaline pumping through my body I clambered out the passenger side door and sprinted past my buddy five metres or so before taking a knee and engaging the targets.

Shouting "Move!" allowing him to break cover and sprint behind me and a further five metres and take a knee, providing covering fire for me to repeat the movement and leap frog behind him.

"Stop firing!" came the order from the DS.

My heart was pounding so hard I thought it was going to burst through my chest. Although this kind of training may not save your life in an ambush situation, it would certainly give you a fighting chance and increase your chances of survival.

NIRTT training over I was now authorised to carry a pistol and that gave me an air of confidence when travelling out and about. I would chauffeur some of the most senior members of the regiment to meetings in Lisburn, Belfast or to our attached roulement squadron at the notorious Maze prison. Preparing to leave camp meant certain procedures had to be followed. I had to sign out with the Ops room and let them know my reason for leaving camp and they would then designate a route before I'd go to the armoury to draw my pistol, and load it at the loading bay. I was always amazed to see the bullet holes in the wall where soldiers over the years had accidentally carried out what is known as a 'negligent discharge' whilst loading or unloading. That would have earned them 15 minutes of fame when their name would be published on the NIREP, NI Report, published daily on routine orders, detailing any shootings or bombings by the IRA, including any negligent discharges.

Armed with a 9mm pistol stuffed down your pants changes your mindset; it heightens your senses and puts you on high alert. The moment you leave the camp gates everyone becomes a suspect and you are constantly aware of your surroundings, always checking the rear view mirror and ensuring you leave a good gap of around a car's length when approaching a junction or traffic lights, always planning an escape route in your mind in case of an ambush.

Northern Ireland is a beautiful country with six counties: Fermanagh, Antrim, Tyrone, Londonderry, Armagh and Down - I would remember them by using the mnemonic phrase, FATLAD. Massereene barracks is in the county of Antrim and sits on the edge of Lough Neagh, Britain's largest lake and an ideal location for our boat and dive teams to be located and deployed from. The camp had two security gates at the main entrance, with the first gate just situated off the main Castle Road, leading to Randallstown, and onto Londonderry. A security tower provided overwatch whilst the guard below would check the occupant's identification before allowing access into the search area where another guard would carry out a detailed vehicle search. The driver would be asked to open his boot and bonnet. Then a mirror on a pole would be used to view the underside for any Vehicle Incendiary Explosive Devices (VIED) which might have been attached to the underside of the vehicle as a means of transporting the device onto a military establishment, usually stuck by a magnet, and normally activated by a timing device, a tactic the IRA used, and often to devastating effect.

The scrap metal man would call in on me during his weekly rounds of the military bases, as I was his point of contact for Massereene barracks, we would have a chat and a brew. He was a pleasant guy, a bit scruffy looking due to the nature of his job, but he also enjoyed a round of golf, and he invited me as his guest to an up and coming competition at Massereene golf club. Dubious at the time as I would be the only military guy amongst a large group of civilians both Protestants and Catholics; it was a precarious time and you needed to be on your guard and suspicious of who you socialised with outside of the camp gates.

My cover story, if asked, was my family owned a scrap metal yard near Liverpool docks, and I was over doing some business – thin, but the best we could come up with, and my host reassured me it would be okay, he would deflect anyone if they were to ask too many questions.

The golf course backed onto our barracks and a familiar setting, so I wasn't too concerned. Back in the clubhouse after the golf and the prize giving I chatted more with my host over a few beers and asked him what made him get into the scrap metal collecting business. It was never his intention, he told me as he had heard how the Provos had issued death threats to any contractors dealing with the military.

"Bloody hell, you must be mad," I said.

He then went on to tell me how he used to be the drummer for a famous Irish showband, and they were having huge success until they were ambushed by the UVF back in 1975 after a gig they had just played in Banbridge, County Down. He had left in his own car and the rest of his band members headed south in their band wagon, they were stopped on the A1 Road in County Down, and out of his fellow bandmates, 3 were killed and 2 were seriously wounded. He now believed he was on borrowed time and if he had been with his fellow bandmates on that fateful night, he would not be standing there drinking a beer with me.

I later went on to join the regimental swimming team and quickly became their number one swimmer. The coach earmarked me for butterfly and medley training, and we trained twice a week for an hour in Antrim's public swimming pool in preparation for the up-and-coming army swimming and water polo championships, being held in Bulford Garrison in Wiltshire in a few weeks' time.

At inter squadron and regimental level I was rarely beaten, but the army championships was another thing altogether as I was soon to find out! The swimming pool at Bulford garrison is Olympic size, a whopping 25 metres and dwarfed the standard 20 metre pool I was used to. It was time for the medley, the big one everyone was looking forward to seeing, and nervously, I stood on the block and took a deep breath, my toes hooked over the front edge for good leverage and to prevent slipping when launching myself off. I remained focused on the race ahead, 200 metres with two lengths of each swimming discipline, starting with the butterfly, followed by the backstroke, then the breaststroke and finally freestyle.

The whistle blew and I was off the blocks with a flying start hitting the water in a shallow dive. I kicked like hell before propelling my head and arms out of the water for the start of the butterfly, a difficult and technical stroke to master. My heart was pounding and the adrenaline was now pumping through my body. I glanced across and could see we were all pretty level in the race and I was swimming the fastest pace of my life, probably due to the adrenaline. At the end of the second turn I began to flag; I felt I was still going strong but had no more gears to go - either I was starting to go backwards or these guys were just getting started. The gap was now increasing as the race went on. By the time we got to the freestyle, these guys were so far ahead they were going in the opposite direction, and by the turn at the end of 7th, I could see all the other swimmers were close to finishing. For a split second I almost gave up, wanting the pool to open up and swallow me whole, but a voice inside my head started screaming "never give up", which was helped along by the crowd spurring me on to finish - not my fastest lap but I got a big cheer when I finished.

Puzzled, I couldn't understand how these guys had thrashed me so easily, and I later found out that these guys were pretty much tracksuit soldiers, spending 4 hours a day, five days a week training, and there was me doing 2 hours a week, eating kebabs and swilling beer most nights - what was I even doing in the same pool as these guys? Cheers, coach!

A trip to the Czech Republic, parachuting, was being organised and volunteers were needed to participate. With no pun intended, I jumped at the chance and a few months later we were off - 4 instructors and eight students. Little did I know that when I signed up for the trip we would be driving there!

Transit van loaded with personal baggage and cooking equipment, we jumped in the minibus, and we're off on a two day journey from Antrim to the Czech Republic - a 1,200 miles stretch of road and two ferry crossings lay ahead.

The first leg, a short drive over to Larne for the ferry crossing to Stranraer, and then by road down to Gibraltar barracks in Camberley, home of the Royal Engineers Sport Parachuting Association (RESPA) and where I had also done my basic training several years earlier. There we had an overnight stop to load up the parachutes and then off we set early next morning to for the Dover to Calais channel crossing and 14 hours later we finally arrived in the early hours of the following morning at Hosin Aeroclub (Aeroklub České Budějovice, Letiště Hosin) close to the town of Ceske Budejovice, about an hour's drive south of Prague.

After a morning's ground training we were ready to jump from an altitude of 3,000 feet connected to a static line - designed to pull your parachute open as you exit the aircraft. Dressed in bright orange jumpsuits and looking like detainees from Guantanamo Bay we boarded the plane, as we all looked at each other like lambs going to the slaughter.

"Next," as the instructor beckoned me to take up position in the doorway.

Dangling your legs out of an open door at 3000ft sends a screaming message to your brain telling it, WTF! Are you serious right now! As the instructor shouts "Jump", your mind goes completely blank and my only recollection after that was dangling in the air under a big canopy. I was later briefed that I shouted, " Holy Sh...t" whilst making cat-like actions trying to climb back into the plane.

After a disastrous and eventful first jump, I managed a further seven and progressed to level 2. On the final day of the trip the chief instructor held a lucky dip and for the winner - a tandem jump from 12,000 feet. My mate won and responded immediately with a "fuck that" he was more than happy to pass the honours over to me. It was after that jump I got hooked on the sport and it set me on my personal quest to become a qualified skydiver.

I attended a few other courses, one of which was a motorcycle instructor's course, 2 weeks in Litchfield scrambling around on Honda 350cc trial bikes, and luckily not the military issued Armstrong 500cc which was a heavy and gutless machine. I also attended my section commander's course which I needed to fully qualify as a corporal and to progress my career further. In what seemed like a blink of an eye my 2-year tour of Northern Ireland had come to an end, and I received a posting order instructing me to report to 21 Engineer Regiment, based in Nienburg, Germany.

Part 8

GERMANY AND BOSNIA

I borrowed Martin's Ford Sierra for the journey from Antrim to Nienburg. I loaded up all my belongings and boarded the ferry from Larne to Stranraer, drove across to Hull and then boarded the overnight ferry to Rotterdam. Later that afternoon I arrived at my new unit. It's always a bit unsettling when your life is piled in the back of a car and you arrive at a unit not knowing anyone, and it normally takes a few days to settle.

I was handed a key for a room which had been allocated for me by the guardroom. The bunk was situated on the top floor and as it was a Friday afternoon. The rest of the camp inmates were already on the piss, with no one about to give me a helping hand, I spent the next few hours lugging my belongings up several flights of stairs and set about unpacking before bedding in for an early night. Laughter and commotion woke me momentarily as drunken soldiers bounced around in the corridor and the familiar drunken banter made me chuckle, but I turned over and went back to sleep as I knew full well now wasn't the best time to introduce myself, having been in that state many times before.

Next morning I woke again early to a knocking and clunking noise in the corridor. Needing the toilet I slipped on a pair of tracksuit bottoms and went to check out the disturbance. I must admit I'm not shocked very easily but being confronted by a disabled woman in a wheelchair 4 storeys up in a building with no lifts was a new one on me. I guess she was in her early 20s.

"You okay," I asked, looking around for Jeremy Beadle to appear.

"I'm gud, danke," she replied, and gestured for me to help her down the stairs. It caught me totally unawares! Unsure what to think of the situation I proceeded to manhandle her in her wheelchair down four flights of stairs and opening the front door, I pushed her out. She wheeled herself off across the drill square waving as she went, and I was left standing there in just my tracksuit bottoms in total disbelief, and thinking what the hell just happened?

The following weekend it was time to get to know the troop and visit a few bars in town. I was long overdue a haircut so I popped into a local barbers, asked for a standard army cut, a short back and sides, please, but unfortunately, he couldn't speak a word of English. My big mistake was in allowing someone to cut my hair when he couldn't understand a word I was saying and the wanker almost took my ears off! I walked out looking like a thug, now sporting a skinhead. We carried on drinking and my new haircut became the topic of the day - it's always best to laugh off banter, otherwise you end up snapping and giving someone a slap.

The boys took me to 'Voices', a local nightclub a short taxi ride from town. The place was buzzing with several bars and a large dance floor. Beers in hand we found a spot to gather overlooking the hundreds of weekend party goers dancing the night away. I couldn't believe my eyes - there she was, centre stage in her wheelchair, bopping away...the disabled woman I had manhandled out of the accommodation block a week earlier; I almost choked on my beer.

As a troop, we quickly began to gel well together and I got on particularly well with my fellow corporal, Al Kilcullen aka "Killer", a quiet guy who had previously served in 59 commando squadron, the Royal Engineers commando squadron based in Barnstaple. We became very good friends, sharing the same passion for motorsports and parachuting.

In 1996 only four months after my arrival, our regiment was relocated to Quebec Barracks in Osnabruck, with the support squadron in which I served being relocated approximately 4 Kilometres away in Roberts Barracks. The Royal Artillery were the main custodians of the camp, and they were not happy to share it with sappers. There has always been a rivalry between us which first came about over the rights to wear the navy-blue lanyard - it's been a long feud between the two corps since World War II. The feud has been battled out on the sports fields over the years, through football and rugby, but a few months after our arrival on camp it almost came to a head in the NAAFI bar one night. As the Gunners dominated one side of the bar, we took our stance and dominated the other. The tension was building throughout the evening and you could have cut the air with a knife it was that thick. Word got round not to leave the bar - it was sure to kick off!

Last orders was called just before midnight and nobody budged. The NAFFI, staff sensing the tension, quickly pulled down the metal shutters and called the guard room. It was now a Mexican standoff - one of our sappers who resembled the Swedish actor, Dolph Lundgren, due to his stature and appearance, stood around 6ft 3in and was built like a brick outhouse, breaking the ice he popped a stack of beer bottle tops on the end of his penis, pulling the skin over and pushed a safety pin through to hold them in place, a party trick he had obviously done before. Stripping off he then stood on the table, muscles bulging and displaying what can only be described as a large battered sausage, and shouted,

"Who wants a sausage fight".

instantly diffused the whole situation, as one of the Gunners piped up, "Fuck that mate, you win," instantly removing the tension in the room, and the night ended without a skirmish.

Our unit had now officially been warned off for a 6 month tour to Bosnia. and with pre deployment training over we flew out to Split in Croatia, before being transported upcountry and across the border into Bosnia as part of the Implementation Force or IFOR as it was better known. It was a six-month winter tour, and our squadron was stationed in an old factory compound near the town of Tomislavgrad, which we abbreviated to TSG, and is situated 900 metres up in a valley of the Bosnian and Herzegovinian mountains. When we arrived at Split airport it was late summer and the weather was warm, but that wasn't to last. The old factory was ideal as it already had a fenced perimeter and a front gate. The main factory unit was utilised as a kitchen and canteen area and ideal for a squadron strength of around 100 soldiers. Our accommodation was situated at the back end of the factory, around twenty Corimec modular containers lined up along the back wall, out of sight from the road which followed the perimeter fence from the side and along the front of the factory. We named it Ocean Drive for 2 reasons, a river of water used to run through during heavy rainfall and it also coincided with the release of the song by the Lighthouse Family and was being continuously played on the British Forces Broadcasting Station channel on the radio. We even named our Corimec and placed a small sign on the door with No1 Ocean Drive, in which the BFBS DJ even paid a visit having heard we had named it after the song.

Within the first week of our arrival the locals from the nearby town saw an opportunity to earn a few quid and cut through the perimeter fence at the back of the vehicle park. They must have been armed with heavy duty cutters as the bastards cut through the battery leads of half our vehicle fleet and made off with the batteries, rendering them off the road for several days. The sergeant major devised a cunning plan and ordered trip flares to be placed around the perimeter fence. He made it the duty corporals' responsibility to arm the flares every evening at 18:00 and to disarm them at 06:00 the following morning. About 20 trip flares in total surrounded the vehicle park and were placed away from any buildings which meant they were exposed to the elements. Setting up a trip flare requires you to lay on your belly, as it contains phosphorus and will cause serious burns if it comes in contact with skin. To remove and replace the safety pin requires lying flat on your stomach and reaching out at arm's length to reduce the risk of a serious burn if it is accidently set off whilst carrying out the task. Sounds easy! However the temperatures in the mountains of Bosnia during the winter months would plummet well below zero and with the ground frozen it made the job extremely difficult. I had done it several times and dreaded it every time, but in fairness it kept the thieving sods away.

The Christmas period that year recorded the lowest temperature at -25 c, with a windchill of -37 c. Our temporary rubber shelter which was our servicing bay was being ripped apart in the storm, and I was tasked with my guys to try and stop it from blowing away. Geared up in as much cold weather clothes as we could get on we attempted to save the shelter. The cold was unbearable and I have never given up on a challenge, but we were not suitably clothed and after several attempts I called it off. The wind and the cold was biting and much to the disapproval of senior management, the safety of my team was my number one priority.

"Fuck the shelter!"

It was badly damaged, but we managed to repair it a few days later.

My guys would often scramble to volunteer whenever a detail down to Split came up, It was a fair old drive down country across the Bosnian border into Croatia, a full day's drive there and back. They seemed too keen and It did raise my curiosity as to why, and it wasn't until I led my first convoy to Split i got the answer. Arriving at the border there were streams of civilian lorries lined up either side of the road waiting to cross, but as we had an RMP presence at the border it allowed us to drive straight down the middle and right up to the checkpoint. As convoy commander I booked in and informed the RMP detachment of our reason for crossing, and how many vehicles and soldiers I had in my convoy. When I entered the small building, and inside I came across the most beautiful female soldier to ever grace an army uniform. Moments later the now small building suddenly became very cramped as half my convoy piled hope to catch a glimpse. RMPs are normally avoided by soldiers, but clearly not on this occasion.

A Christmas parcel arrived from home; mum had sent some goodies - my favourite shortbread biscuits, a few chocolate bars and a Santa hat with a flashing light that blinkered on and off! The sergeant major decided it only fair the sappers and lance corporals who normally carry out all the guard duties should be stood down on Christmas Day and New Year's Eve, and the guard shifts would be done by full corporals and above. I was pinged for the midnight shift on New Year's Eve and standing next to the gate wearing my Father Christmas hat blinking away, weapon in hand and staring out into the pitch darkness, a distant noise began getting closer from the direction of town. Soon headlights appeared around the corner as a stream of cars and pickup trucks headed up the road towards me alongside the perimeter fence. Just at the stroke of midnight, the sky was suddenly lit with tracer rounds being fired from AK47 and various other weapons, as the procession of vehicles passed me by. Men were cheering and shouting with weapons pointing skywards as they hung out the vehicle windows and unloaded their magazines of live rounds in celebration. I decided the safest option was to step behind the concrete gate pillar which was no wider than the width of an average tree trunk, praying it would offer me some protection if a drunken idiot was to lose control of his weapon and point it in my direction. I was glad it was a passing celebration and not a full scale attack, as most of the squadron was half pissed and I only had 10 rounds of ammunition!

After the Dayton Peace Accord had been signed the Implementation Force (IFOR) role in which we had been deployed now changed to a more peaceful Stabilization Force known as SFOR. Troop strength and numbers began to draw down. I was tasked as convoy commander, responsible for the collection of engineer stores from around our theatre of operations. Covering a large area, my team of heavy goods vehicles and drivers travelled the length and breadth of Bosnia and Herzegovina collecting stores, including bridging equipment, back to the port of Split in Croatia.

There I was assigned an attachment of Ghurkhas to move 20 or so shipping containers. The containers had been loaded and brought to our location in TSG by various other units, packed and lined up ready to be transported. The attachment of Gurkhas arrived in 14t Bedford flatbed trucks, ideal for shipping containers as the bed of the vehicles have a locking bolt at each corner; with a turn of a pin the container is secured firmly to the vehicle - no need for straps or chains.

It was now around 7pm. I briefed the Gurkha commander on their arrival, and he in turn briefed his men. The brief was simple. They were to remain in their vehicles, and when called forward my team would carry out the loading and securing. The process was running smoothly, until disaster struck. The crane manoeuvred a container into position on the rear of the vehicle. With the locking pins secured, the slinger was now on top of the loaded container about to unhook the chains, when the crane operator beeped his horn to grab the attention of another team member. The Gurkha driver took this as a signal to move off, and did so at such speed and completely unaware that he was still attached to the crane, and with one of my guys still 15 feet up on the back of his vehicle. He jumped for his life and was lucky to land with only minor injuries. The crane was pulled up sideways and the crane operator also jumped and scrambled for cover as the crane raised up on its side before crashing back down, causing extensive damage. Luckily nobody was seriously injured, except for the wrath of fucks I fired into the Gurkha driver and his commander.

Our squadron's interpreter, who we nicknamed Baz, was from Vitez in Central Bosnia, a town badly affected by ethnic cleansing 2 years earlier and was due her R&R. I was detailed to make sure she was taken home safely. My driver and I, in the lead vehicle, followed by an escort vehicle, arrived at Baz's house and were greeted by her parents. Her father insisted on inviting me in. They spoke no English but Baz told me it would be rude to refuse. Almost every house and building had been damaged or destroyed in the area. Not one to offend, I instructed the escort vehicle to wait outside as I went inside with my driver. A plate of sliced salami was placed on the table and Baz's father offered me a drink using the multinational sign language we all understand. With a quick nod I was handed a large bottle of Pivo, whilst my driver was handed a hot drink of what looked like stewed tea. I ordered him not to be rude and made sure he drank it all. Later he was calling me all the names under the sun, telling me it tasted like cat's piss. It was a strange feeling sitting in someone's bullet riddled home, with a pistol in my holster and a rifle across my lap, drinking 8% beer and eating some sliced leather.

Operational tours have a no alcohol policy, but since the war in Bosnia had ended the policy was relaxed a little, soldiers were entitled to a drink. A two can rule when off duty was introduced, although the policy makers never stipulated the size of can and two 20 litre Jerrycans hung behind our bar to remind us of the policy. Sappers are renowned for taking things one step too far!

Back in Germany it was time for some well-earned adventure training and a group of us soon arrived at Sapper Lodge in Bavaria. First port of call is always to dump your bag on a vacant bed to claim it and then check out the bar. I couldn't believe my eyes when from behind the bar popped up my old sergeant major - yes, the old fucker who punished me on my arrival at Waterbeach years earlier. He was now a civilian and running the lodge.

"Remember me?" I said.

"Of course I do. Here's a free pint, and don't hit me," he said jokingly, explaining how he was a power crazed sergeant major back then and admitted how he took bullying a bit far at times. He wasn't a bad fella - it was just how it was.

The Quartermaster, an old crusty major, tagged along and enjoyed a few beers with the boys. He and I got on like a house on fire. He placed himself in my training group, telling me how he wanted to chill out and that I was still the group leader.

"Corporal Roberts, just tell me when and where I should be," he said.

"Yes sir, no problem, I'll look after you."

Hiking around the Bavarian mountains, the last thing you expect to hear is the sound of an oompah band

"Corporal Roberts, where there's music there's beer."

"I hear you, sir," I replied, sprinting over the brow of the next hill and shouting back at the old man, "last one there gets the first round in".

It was the height of summer and there in front of me, a 1000 ft up, overlooking the valley below and filled with fellow hikers enjoying a stein of beer and slapping their thighs, was just what the doctor ordered.

Back at the lodge as I strolled in, three sheets to the wind, I was confronted by my squadron 2i/c. We never did see eye to eye, and realising I was a bit pissed he chose this moment to give me a bit of a rollocking; that was until my saviour came bouncing off the corridor walls behind me, putting the young captain back in his box...for now!

I bought myself a tax-free motorbike, a brand-new Honda CBR600, but soon found myself in a German hospital with 16 pins in my left scapula after misjudging a sweeping left hander and somersaulting down the road at 90 miles an hour. I decided to give up the dangerous motorbikes and returned to skydiving!

I attended a basic parachuting jumps course at the Rhine Army Parachuting centre (RAPA) at Bad Lippspringe in Paderborn. It was a progression style course, designed to take you through category levels from 1 to 8. Level 1 starts you on a static line from 3000 feet, up to level 8, which is around 50 seconds of freefall from 12,000 feet and is free to all serving personnel. The alternative is a far quicker course called accelerated freefall (AFF) but that would have set me back around £1,000 at the time.

By the end of the second week, I had achieved 15 jumps and attained level 4. and I was more determined than ever to reach level 8. I would travel down on weekends and pay for my own jumps and the hire of equipment. I was creeping closer to my goal or becoming a level 8 qualified skydiver. Looking back, I should have just paid the £1,000. Then the bombshell came; I received a short notice posting order to report to 22 Engineer Regiment in Tidworth in three weeks' time. I was gutted. It was courtesy of my old favourite squadron 2i/c; the smug look on his face said it all as he took great pleasure informing me. Unfortunately my saviour could not help me this time.

Before my departure from Germany, my troop gave me several send offs, including dining out in a great little restaurant somewhere out of town. A 12 seater minibus did a double trip to drop us all off, and at the entrance to the restaurant was a large fish tank with 2 lobsters, a nice front of house feature. There was the usual evening of food, drinks and speeches and at the end of the evening the minibus had gone off on its first run with the younger members of the troop, when the restaurant owner approached our table, and informed us his 2 prize lobsters had gone AWOL from front of house. My initial reaction was to act dumb, but my squaddie brain knew immediately what had happened. I decided to keep the peace and paid the owner 100 deutsche marks, about £40, as a good gesture not to call the polizei. After plenty of apologies and handshakes the owner seemed content to drop the matter. Back at the accommodation block I climbed the flight of stairs and could hear what sounded like a day at the races. On entering the corridor I was greeted with a dozen drunken guys on their knees screaming at 2 lobsters to race along the corridor - the poor fuckers never lasted the night!

BOSNIA - CONVOY COMMANDER

BOSNIA - ON GUARD
NEW YEARS EVE

BOSNIA - FANCY DRESS NIGHT (SHOWADDYWADDY)

CALIFORNIA - LAKE ELSINOR DZ (NOTE DC 10 IN BACKGROUND)

CALIFORNIA - PARACHUTING
(PREPARING TO FLARE FOR LANDING)

CALIFORNIA - LANDED

Part 9

TIDWORTH 98/01

Every cloud has a silver lining. I reported for duty to 22 Engineer Regiment and after a bit of a mix up with my assignment I was eventually given my role as the Military Transport Corporal (MT Cpl), and after a few months settling in I read on routine orders,

'Calling all wanna be skydivers. An allocation of 30 beginners or novices required to participate in a parachuting exercise being organised by the Corps parachuting team to California'.

Without hesitation I put my name in the hat and paid the £300-pound individual contribution fee; luckily, I had just come from Germany where beer was cheap, so I had plenty of spare cash. The extra money was being contributed from the regimental sports pot, a no brainer considering flights alone were somewhere in the region of £600.

I was in, but, there was a but! My OC called me into his office and placed a caveat on releasing me for the trip, he explained how he would allow me to go, on the understanding that I attended a bridging course on my return. He went on to explain there was a new bridging system which had recently been signed off by the British

Army Trials Team and was being rolled out to all general support units of the Royal Engineers, and he wanted me to be our first ABLE Commander. I must admit, I felt privileged and it was a fair trade off, but all I was thinking at the time was, just get me on that damn plane!

Approximately 36 of us including instructors arrived at Gibraltar barracks the day before we were due to fly. After a briefing by the chief instructor we loaded our parachutes into a van which was to follow us to Heathrow the following morning. On arrival at check-in the chief instructor asked us to double-check our parachutes and ensure the automatic opening devices were switched off, as it could be carnage for the baggage handlers on landing if devices automatically popped open 36 reserve parachutes. The device known as a "Cypres" is an automatic activation device and will open the parachute in the event a skydiver is knocked unconscious or is unable to open his main parachute. It operates if it falls through a low altitude at a speed of over 80 mph, safer to hit the ground at 25 mph with a headache and a few bruises, than piling into the ground at 120mph.

A voice suddenly pipped up, a young 2nd lieutenant.

"Excuse me, chief, where's my parachute?"

He had decided to meet us at the airport and assumed his parachute would have been loaded and packed for him - assumption being the mother of all fuck ups should have been this young officer's first lesson in leadership! But to his credit, he did show great initiative in managing to persuade a fellow officer from Gib barracks to grab a parachute and meet him halfway, and he eventually managed to make the flight.

On board the Virgin Trans-Atlantic flight to Los Angeles was a free bar, and the flight attendants had their work cut out, trying to meet the continuous demands for free alcohol to a large group of thirsty squaddies, to the point that they told us to just help ourselves. We soon drank the plane dry and upset some of the civilian passengers trying to sleep - sorry guys but a free bar is a free bar!

We arrived some 10 hrs later at Los Angeles LAX airport. Blurry eyed and 3 sheets to the wind we gathered our gear and made our way over to the vehicle hire car company. The chief instructor looked around and posed two questions: firstly,

"Who's got their driving licence? and secondly, "who is sober enough to drive?"

A slight oversight not covered during the initial brief! After some panic as to who was able to drive, we set off in several small seven-seater carryall vehicles, crammed to the hilt with bodies, parachutes and personal baggage and headed off to Lake Elsinore. Two hours later we finally arrived at the Casino Hotel, where we would be staying for the next two weeks and only a five-minute drive from the drop zone (DZ).

Our party was made up of varying levels of parachuting experience, from beginners who had never jumped to novices like me who had a few jumps under their belts. The instructors were all experienced skydivers with hundreds, and some with thousands, of jumps and having competed in competitions all over the world. In fact one of them had just competed in the Australian championships. One of the beginners was well over 6ft tall and weighed around 20 stone, a big lad and needed the biggest parachute available, but like all beginners he was nervous as hell. He had reason to be as he had a malfunction on his first jump; his main parachute didn't fully open, but with excellent training he still had the awareness to cut away and land safely. A cutaway is a drill carried out when you look up and see your lines are tangled, and your canopy has not deployed correctly, or is damaged. A cord is then pulled which detaches the main parachute from the container and deploys the reserve.

This is a terrifying experience, and a rare occurrence to happen to someone on their very first jump, but with encouragement from the rest of the team we managed to persuade the big man to jump again the next morning, telling him that a malfunction twice in a row is unheard of and the chances of it happening again must be at least a million to one. The poor bastard should have bought a lottery ticket - he defied all the odds and malfunctioned again on his second jump. No amount of encouragement was going to get this guy to don a parachute and jump ever again.

Meanwhile my personal goals were being met and by the end of the first week I obtained my level 8. I was now a qualified skydiver, literally on cloud 9 and just in time for the weekend stand down. Chief gave us all a 2-day rest from skydiving for some R+R. Vehicles were designated to go to various destinations, San Francisco, Vegas, LA, and Tijuana in Mexico. I opted to go with the crazy bunch to Tijuana.

We set off on the scenic route and drove to Santa Monica to check out Baywatch's female lifeguards and Hollywood boulevard for a quick photo shoot, before heading down the famous Interstate 5 to San Diego. We couldn't resist popping into McDonalds for lunch at the naval air station, Miramar, made famous by Tom Cruise in the 1986 film Top Gun. With a flash of our army I.D cards we were soon queuing up for a big Mac and chips when two fighter pilots dressed in their pilot suits and wearing mirrored sunglasses strutted past. They went straight to the front of the queue, removing their sunglasses and chewing gum, stopping everyone in their tracks as people stared in awe. Then a British voice from our party shouted,

"Oi! Cheeky bastards, haven't you heard of queuing?" when one of the customers muttered,

"Hey man, they're Top Gun". She explained that a perk to being an elite fighter pilot is they don't queue, and to be honest, it's a fair shout.

We parked states-side, crossing the border into Mexico by foot on a 24 hour visa. A short taxi ride into Tijuana and we pulled up outside a slummy hotel on the main high street. The hotel receptionist was enclosed behind steel bars, the type you see in a sheriff's office in old spaghetti westerns. We dumped our bags in the room and hit the bars. It was now late afternoon and the streets were bustling and quickly filling up. and on every street corner was a police pickup truck with two armed policemen riding shotgun and carrying automatic rifles. We all looked at each other and one lad suggested we stick close together; nods of acknowledgement all round showed that we certainly agreed that this was a bloody good idea!

We entered a bar where scantily clad females were strutting about everywhere, music was blaring and for ten dollars you could have a private lap dance in a designated area set aside from the bar area and guarded by a large bouncer. Ten dollars later and two of us were led over towards the bouncer. A small fence segregated the area from the rest of the room, no more than a foot high, and I chuckled as the bouncer bent down to open the gate. Our dancer entered first, followed closely by my mate. The bouncer stopped me by putting his hand to my chest and shutting the gate.

"Only one at a time," he said.

I turned around, disappointed and headed back to our table feeling dejected. Looking across and watching my mate I could see him smirking at me as he was enjoying his lap dance. But I had the last laugh when a few moments later his cheesy grin turned into a somewhat bewildered look as it was revealed to him that this lovely young lady was actually a he. Leaping from his chair and over the tiny fence he quickly marched back to our table telling me,

"Drink up quick, we're leaving". I was pissing myself as he asked me to promise not to mention it to anyone.

Back in the UK it was time to honour my deal with the OC and I soon found myself back at Gibraltar barracks on a six week pilot bridging course. With a 10 man bridging team we were capable of launching a 32 metre, class 70 tank bridge in around 30 minutes. The Automotive Bridge Launching Equipment known as ABLE consisted of three 38 tonne out of gauge vehicles: two vehicles carrying the bridging panels, and the third provided an extended building platform from which to launch the bridge. After I successfully passed both the bridging operator and commander phase of the course, I was now one of only a handful of ABLE Commanders in the Corps of the Royal Engineers and responsible for our unit's two complete bridging sets and the only person in the unit at the time qualified to launch this multi-million-pound assets. I soon became the OC's number one soldier, and he couldn't wait to show off his squadron's bridging capability.

On the afternoon of Thursday 21st of January, 1999, I received a message to report to the OC's office urgently.

"Afternoon sir, another bridging demo?" I asked. "Not this time Cpl Roberts. There's been a serious air collision involving an RAF Tornado and a small civilian plane."

It's the responsibility of the Royal Engineers to provide support to the RAF in such events, and a job normally given to an SNCO. "I want you to get one of your drivers and jump in a Land Rover and get yourself up there as fast as you can, and provide assistance"

We arrived at the crash site in Nottinghamshire 4 hours later just as it began to get dark. We could just see a small detachment of RAF guys along with around a dozen police officers who were now heading back across a large open field towards us and carrying plastic bags, and in the field in the distance I could just make out a large round object.

I reported to the RAF SNCO in charge and introduced myself. He gave me a brief run down on the situation, A Tornado GR1 was on a routine training flight from RAF Cottesmore and collided with a Cessna, a light aircraft with 2 occupants onboard. We later found out they were flying over the village nearby photographing properties in the area when the collision happened, and came crashing down 200 yards away from a primary school near Mattersey, around 3 km down the road. The Tornado was piloted by an Italian Air Force pilot with an RAF pilot instructor as passenger. Such was the speed and force of the collision that the Tornado crashed down here, approximately 11 miles from Doncaster - all four were killed.

"How can I assist?", I asked. "I need the muddy section of access laying with hardcore." Not a problem and I estimated I needed around a 100 tons of aggregate for the job. While he set about ordering the hardcore for immediate delivery, I phoned my OC and requested 2 of our military tipper trucks, a JCB loader and compactor be sent up to the site. The RAF SNCO kindly arranged accommodation for the 2 of us in the nearest military establishment as the aggregate and equipment we needed wouldn't be arriving until the next morning.

I arrived on site early the next morning, to find that daybreak had revealed a clear view of the devastation of the crash site. The large round object I had seen the previous night was one of the main engines, the only recognisable part left of the plane - the rest lay in bits strewn over a half mile area of field.

As I looked over the crash site, I couldn't help but wonder whether the pilot had been still alive after the initial impact and had deliberately avoided the nearby villages, or was it just luck that the Tornado landed in a large open field? Could he have ejected? Who knows, I would like to think the selfless bravery of these pilots deliberately avoided catastrophe by purposely ditching it in the open field.

As the aggregate was being stockpiled, and my guys arrived on-site, I knew I needed this job to go well. I was a senior corporal doing a task usually delegated to an SNCO; it would be a big tick in the box for me on the next promotion board. I briefed my drivers and told them the speed limit on-- site was no more than 15 mph; it was January and the ground was icy and frozen solid. The first tipper loaded and he set off like a bloody lunatic and slipped off the country lane and into the ditch. I was gobsmacked and within seconds I was legging it down the road towards him as he was getting out of the vehicle which was now leaning precariously to one side with a full load of aggregate on board. I cried out,

"You fucking twat," at which he quickly decided to get back in the cab and lock the doors.

Lucky for him, the second tipper was able to recover his vehicle without tipping over, but he sensibly made sure to give me a wide berth for the remainder of the task.

The following year I returned to California. I had done a few jumps back in the UK at the Joint Service Parachuting Centre at Netheravon, near Salisbury, just enough to keep my hand in the game. But now I was starting what is known in the skydiving world as WARP training, learning how to fly my body in freefall. It's a progression from level 8 to a level 10 qualification and would allow me to participate in larger formation skydives.

I practised hard on my drills, and soon it was time for me to take my level 10 qualifying jump. An American guy arrived at the drop zone (DZ), invited by one of our military instructors who had met him during a recent major championship event. He was one of the skydiving coaches for The Golden Knights, the elite United States military skydiving team. He asked to join me on my level 10 qualifying jump, adding extra pressure for me to perform with one of the best skydiving coaches in the world.

We exited the aircraft from 12,000 feet as a four-way formation, the aim - to gain the minimum four-point manoeuvre whilst keeping the formation tight. It is very easy to drift apart once you release your grip on the formation. The idea is to release your grip and rotate either 45, 90 or 180 degrees and then reconnect with the formation, not so simple when falling to earth at 120mph. Once you start to drift you can be 10 feet away from the formation as you rotate at the same time as you are quickly losing altitude. Luckily, the extra pressure worked and I nailed it with ten points; my dream of becoming a fully-fledged category 10 skydiver had now become a reality.

An old DC3 aircraft used in Hollywood films landed in the small airfield and I don't know how it came about but all the category 10 skydivers were given the chance to jump out of it. Newly qualified, I was not going to miss this golden opportunity to jump out of such an iconic plane, which was first used to drop paratroopers behind enemy lines in 1942. One of the skydivers had developed a problem with his ear and not wanting to miss out on this historic jump, asked if he could jump out at an altitude of just 5,000ft. The chief instructor watched him go out the door and immediately turned his head in horror, realising immediately that the pilot had not reduced the thrust on the propeller on that side. The skydiver came within inches of hitting the rear tail fin as the airflow from the huge propeller pushed the skydiver backward almost parallel with the plane and would have almost certainly killed him. The pilot was not at fault as the plane had not been used by paratroopers for over 50 years, so it was fortunate that his ear problem averted a potential disaster for the rest of us.

A few more American skydivers arrived at the DZ, and the Golden Knights' coach set about organising a large freefall formation. He gathered together all those qualified to take part and started orchestrating a 28-way formation. He briefed us first before walking us through it on the ground; that enables you to visualise the jump in your mind and allows you to identify your position in the formation by varied coloured jumpsuits.

Two aircraft now loaded with skydivers took to the sky, and at 14,000 feet above the DZ we were flying parallel to each other around 100 ft apart and the green light to jump lit up. My heart pounding with excitement, we scrambled out of the plane one after the other, almost on top of each other, desperate to get out and get into formation. I could see the other jumpers falling out of the other plane, a spectacular sight, the sky was full of different coloured bodies as I slowed my rate of descent by de-arching my body, which allowed me to look down below and find my slot. I flew sideways around the formation, cautious not to fly over the top as the dead airflow from the formation can cause you to accelerate your descent rapidly and bomb into the formation, and make you a very unpopular figure. I saw my slot and circled around and swooped in, grabbed the legs of the 2 coloured jumpsuits I had imprinted on my mind during the walkthrough and successfully formed our pod within the formation. It felt electrifying; 28 bodies were now joined together as one, falling to earth at over 120mp. It was exhilarating to say the least. With the formation complete we burned a hole in the sky for a few thousand feet before peeling off. This is probably the most dangerous part of the jump, the separation and canopy pull, the outer ring of the formation releases and turns first, 180 degrees and away from the formation at a predetermined altitude, tracking as far away as possible into clear airspace before banging on a hard arch to slow down and open your parachute. I released my grip, turned and burned across the sky, holding my track for about 10 seconds, then banged on a hard arch, throwing open my parachute. Moments later the sky was littered with parachutes, a spectacular sight and the sounds of "Yahoos" echoed all around - the Americans' way of saying, "Good job!"

The weather took a turn for the worse, so a decision was made to move up to the Nevada Desert and check into a hotel in Laughlin, a gambling town 90 miles south of Vegas, The accommodation was cheap and clean. Gambling hotels rely on their revenue from slot machines. Leaving the hotel next morning at 07:00 I noticed a middle-aged lady sat playing a slot machine opposite the hotel lift, and I couldn't believe she was still there when we returned after dark the same day. Our remaining days in California were spent skydiving in the desert by day and soaking up the atmosphere in hotel bars and casinos at night; I was on top of the world.

I finally realised it was time to grow up and think about settling down, a tough choice when you're on a roll and enjoying life. I was now 29 and still a corporal. Everyone I knew was already either married or settled. I met Clare when she was an 18-year-old barmaid in a local pub whilst home on R&R from Bosnia back in 1996, just over two years ago, and on my return from California I decided to bite the bullet and proposed. I offered her a Caribbean wedding; I guess I didn't want all the fuss. I love a good wedding but only when the attention is on other people. I must admit I was taken aback when she said yes, but even more surprised when she turned down a Caribbean wedding, opting for a registry office wedding in Rhyl instead. A date was set and with my best man, Al, by my side we got hitched on the 20th of February 1999, with only a handful of family and friends present. The landlady at the Masons put on a spread and with the Six Nations Wales v Scotland game showing on the television in the pub it made for a great day that we all enjoyed.

We soon settled into married quarters in Tidworth, a month prior to my squadron being deployed for my second tour to Bosnia. As a newlywed I was granted 3 months on rear party. It felt strange not being part of the squadron as I settled into cosy nights with the new missus, and if the truth be known I was craving to be back with my squadron in Bosnia after a few weeks...it's a squaddie thing.

Three months later my wish came true; I was to fly out and join my squadron. Clare was understandably upset but the hard truth was that it was something she would have to get used to. Being a military wife is tough, away from their families and the husband away on operations, they become dependent on the military network. For newlywed wives new to the system I suspect it is very daunting.

I packed my Bergan and kit bag and loaded up the car for Clare to take me the mile or so up to camp and drop me off early on the day of my departure. She cried and was upset, and as we pulled up to the camp gates I told her to just pull up by the gate and swing round. I gave her a quick kiss and told her I would be home before she knew it, and got out of the car. As I walked around to the boot to grab my kit, she drove off in an upset state leaving me standing at the camp gates with no kit. The 2 soldiers on the gate pissed themselves with laughter and I couldn't bollock them as I would have done the same, but with no mobile phone I had to wake up the duty driver to drive me back home to collect my gear.

Gornji Vakuf, a disused metal factory in central Bosnia, seemed a much more peaceful place since my last deployment. You could sense the country was returning to some sort of normality. After only 4 weeks my squadron was ordered to vacate Gornji Vakuf and redeploy to Split in Croatia for the remainder of the tour, as the drawdown increased. Two months of slipper city here we come. The 2 can rule was out the window and the only restriction placed on us was a midnight curfew. The historic harbour town of Trogir became our escape, a short taxi ride with a few mates and I was sipping beer and eating pizza, soaking up the sun on the beautiful Adriatic coast - meanwhile we were telling the wives back home we were having a terrible time!

In Early 2000, I was back at Gibraltar barracks on an advanced bridging course, another six weeks commanding my team on long span and two span bridging. The equipment was extremely complex and mind-boggling, but again I managed to successfully complete the course and become a well-known figure in the field. Deploying on exercise, it was time to put my bridging skills to the test and during a 2 week exercise my team and I grew more and more frustrated at our superiors' lack of knowledge and their misunderstanding of how we were to be utilised. Commanders on the ground were not used to working with the complexity and understanding of the bridge's capabilities, which caused a lot of confusion. Time and time again I would try and explain what had to be done, and at times I felt as though they thought I was being an awkward bugger, when in fact I was trying to educate them. After all this is what training was all about. By the end of the 2 weeks, the final assault was underway, the regiment had crossed my bridge and our task for the next 24hrs was to guard over the bridge site. The crossing point was known as Bravo Crossing, a well-known and prominent point on Salisbury plain. I briefed my 2ic to set up a harbour area, get the vehicles camouflaged and get the stag rota going. Six of us remained at the site so I elected to be included in the rota, 1 guy on stag every hour giving everyone a good 5 hours downtime. As dawn began to break during my stag, a tall figure of a man, around 50 years old appeared from nowhere. He started to approach me, walking across the bridge. He was in military uniform without headdress and his hands were tucked in his combat jacket. Instinctively I could tell he was an ex-ranking officer though he wasn't wearing any insignia. Instead of the usual "halt who goes there" bollocks, I just said

"Good morning, can I help you?"

"Morning corps," he said, cementing my instinct that he wasn't mainstream. He introduced himself as a captain with the pathfinders, a specialised reconnaissance platoon of the parachute brigade, and carrying out surveillance training in the area.

"I've had a team observing you from a hide no more than 50 yards from where we are standing, observing your every movement over the last 6 hours" he told me.

He wanted to know if any of us had any inclination that they were being watched, a great way of getting feedback. I replied,

"Nothing has been mentioned during our stag handovers, so I reckon not sir".

His parting words were, "Good, and tell the small one in your team to dig a hole next time he takes a shit," which made me chuckle.

Morning routine - wake up my team, fill up the boiling vessel (BV) with water, pop in a breakfast ration pack and within 10 minutes there was enough hot water for a brew and a wash and shave, and a hot ready meal. The breakfast ration pack came in a silver foil-like packet which you rip along the top and delve in with a spoon, mostly beans with a couple of slices of sausage and bacon thrown in. Having a BV was one of the perks of being in a vehicle during exercise. It makes the morning routine a lot easier than sleeping under a basha In the woods and heating up a mess tin of water with hexamine blocks. Also having the comfort of a vehicle seat to eat your food, instead of getting your arse wet sitting on a log in the middle of a wooded area is always an added bonus.

The CO and his driver arrived soon after breakfast. I was napping in the vehicle at the time when one of my guys came and woke me up, saying,

"The Colonel's here. He wants to speak to you".

The Colonel was a big fella, an imposing figure with a big moustache, who later rose to the rank of 3-star general. I quickly called my team together and prepared myself to get my pants pulled down; I had shown some contempt and frustration over the last 2 weeks towards senior commanders and felt I was about to get an arse chewing from the big man.

"Cpl Roberts, you and your team have been the only ones to have impressed me during this whole exercise, and I want to personally thank each and every one of you for your hard work, patience and commitment throughout."

He went on to explain that the failures during the exercise was a steep learning curve for his commanders to now take on board and learn from. He took me to one side and informed me that he was strongly recommending me for promotion to Sergeant. I was blown away by what he had just said. I now know when commanding officers are writing their annual reports on their soldiers, the word 'strongly' placed in front of recommended for promotion is a key buzz word informing the promotion board to look closer at this soldier. True to his word, some months later I received a call from him informing me I had been selected for promotion to Sergeant, and soon after I received a posting order as a troop Sergeant to 1 Royal School of Military Engineering (RSME) based in Chatham in Kent.

Part 10

CHATHAM 01/03

I was now working in an office with a desk and a white square box they call a computer. I was now 32 years old and 'Battlestar Galaxia' in the arcades in Rhyl during my young teenage years was the only prior experience I had with computers. The military spent thousands of pounds training me to become a fully qualified bridging specialist to then promote me to desk jockey! And with Clare now pregnant with twins my whole life was about to change, so a stable posting probably suited our current situation. However, that was not before entering the Tri Service Army Parachuting Championships.

I was part of a 4-way team made up of a female army officer, and two soldiers from the parachute regiment pathfinders. Our first day's training jump went reasonably well, and we were keen to make good small mistakes at the start of the competition the following day. Unfortunately it wasn't to be as the two pathfinders received notice to return immediately to their unit and were immediately deployed to Sierra Leone as part of the rescue operation to free the Irish Rangers who had been taken hostage by The West Side Boys, Codenamed Operation Barras.

I was now without a team, so I entered into the solo accuracy competition - the idea is to hop and pop out of the aeroplane from around 3,000 ft, open your parachute once clear of the aircraft, and lining yourself up into the wind to land on a small inflatable target roughly the size of a large garden paddling pool, with the centre of the target gaining the most points. The most points gained over 4 attempts is the winner. Admittedly I was fucking useless, I missed the target by a country mile on my first 3 attempts, saving my best till last, but I overshot the target, missing by a few feet, and ended the competition with 'nil pwa'.

The following year I managed to enter the competition again, and this time I had my best mate , Al, to join me for his first time competing in the competition. It was a disappointment overall as it ended up as a bit of a washout with us only managing a couple of jumps together. Our most memorable jump almost ended in disaster. We carried out the usual pre-boarding checks, checking each other over to make sure we had donned our parachutes correctly, legs were in the leg straps, pull toggle was accessible and the automatic opening device was switched on. With a quick thumbs up from everyone we boarded the plane and headed for the sky; nothing unusual so far, but as we reached 12,000 feet the pilot was radioed and informed to hold off, as a helicopter was below and coming into land.

Netheravon is also home to a small military helicopter detachment. We circled around for a bit, and then gestured for the pilot to go higher whilst we waited for the helicopter to clear off. He eventually climbed to an altitude of 18,500 feet and in a non-pressurised aircraft you start to feel the effects of hypoxia, light-headedness and sickness. I couldn't wait to get out the door as I was starting to feel pretty light headed. The green light came on and the all clear to jump was given. Al and I excited the aircraft with no pre-jump routine, we just flew around bumping into each other and generally just having a good crack. I can still picture him now with his crazy rubber face, even more exaggerated in freefall - you know that face that a dog has when it sticks its head out of a moving car window. I could see he wasn't checking his altimeter, and with an open hand I gestured to him that we were at 5,000 ft. He waved back, I wasn't sure if it was an acknowledgement or he was just waving back, and a few seconds later we were at 3500 feet. I signalled to AL to turn and burn, waving my hands across each other in front of my face before I turned and burned. I was now under the canopy at the recommended height of around 2,500ft and looking down I could see "Al" still doing somersaults and dicking around. Powerless to do anything, I started to fear the worst, then moments later his parachute began to open, hundreds of feet below me. Thank God, I thought.

On the ground we joked about the jump, and I asked him,

"What altitude did you pull at?".

With a snigger he replied,

"Too bloody low!"

As we laughed it off, knowing full well between us that it wasn't a smart move, we gathered up our canopies and made our way across the DZ, and through check-in. But he was pulled to one side by a member of the ground crew and informed how everyone gasped when they heard his parachute open. From the ground you can hear parachutes opening quietly above you; clearly the loud noise Al's canopy made when it opened grabbed the attention of everyone on the ground so he must have been pretty low.

The recommended height is to allow time for a skydiver to react in the event of a malfunction: it gives you a short time to make a quick assessment as to whether you can deal with a problem such as twisted lines, which can be easily undone by kicking your legs and spinning around; or whether it's something more sinister like a streamer, where the canopy has failed to open, and you have time and altitude to cut it away and deploy your reserve. He estimated that he pulled it at around 1700 feet and was under canopy by around 1500 feet. Any lower and the automatic opening devices would have been activated. He received a warning and was grounded for the rest of the day. It was the last time we had the opportunity to parachute together, and he certainly made it a memorable one. I had now completed over 150 parachute jumps but due to a young family to support I gave up the sport.

Back at Chatham life started to slow. I took up golf again and in November 2001 my twin daughters, Jade and Cayla were born. I was now the proud father of two beautiful girls. I felt that I needed a new challenge and jumped at the opportunity when I was asked if I wanted to take part in Trailwalker, a 100km charity event which took place annually across the South Downs, raising money for Oxfam. The event began in 1981 as a military training exercise for the elite Queen's Gurkha Signals Regiment in Hong Kong, but when Hong Kong was handed over to China in 1997 it was reestablished in Britain in 2002. A team of 4 of us decided to take part the following year. We began training a couple of 2 hour sessions a week, building up to 4 hours training runs every Sunday. We raised the £2000 needed to enter the race and left Chatham for Petersfield with our driver and minibus as our support crew. We made our way to the start line with around a hundred or so other competitors where The Blue Peter presenter, Peter Duncan, did the honours as starter. After wishing everyone good luck, he fired the starting gun and we were off. Within 20 minutes we had broken free and were now ahead of the group. Our plan was to run for 4 hours and play the rest by ear. Fifty kilometres in and we were flying, but the next 50km and the brakes began to come on, each of us in turn suffering at varying distances. The weather for July was horrendous, the team dug deep and finally crossed the line in Brighton in 17 hours and 13 minutes. My legs were in bits and blood was seeping through the top of my trainers; all 4 of us decided to leave them on until we got back home as we piled into the back of the minibus and crashed out for the duration of the journey home. The sun was just rising as we arrived in Chatham and our driver dropped each of us off at home. He even helped us to our front doors as our legs had seized up and our feet were wrecked. Once inside I took a deep breath and held it as I peeled my trainers and socks off, and 9 of my 10 toenails promptly dropped on the carpet. The pain of raw flesh being exposed to the air was like stubbing a toe 9 times!

By now, Al had been seeing Sue, the sister of my Jif lemon-yielding mate from back home for a couple of years, and their relationship was blossoming. You will remember that they met when Al first came to Denbigh with me for a piss-up after our tour in Bosnia. Sue worked in the Mason's Arms pub, the local I used to drink in whenever I was home, and the two of them hit it off right away. They soon grew close, and married in 2002 and I was honoured when asked to be his best man.

British forces were now deployed in a war in the middle east, while I was still busy trying to work out a bloody computer by day and surrounded by soiled nappies at night. I probably should have been grateful, but deep down I was frustrated. Like most soldier I wanted to be part of the action, and felt I was missing out. Instead, I was tasked with arranging military educational visits to London once a month for the young soldiers in my troop. A coach load of us, along with my corporals, visited the Imperial War Museum, and on arrival I impressed on them the need to spend at least two hours in the museum, and to ensure they did so I told them I would be nominating a few individuals after the trip to write an article for our corp's much loved Sapper Magazine. I also impressed on them that the coach would depart at 19:00 hours sharp, and if missed, big boys rule applied, and they would have to find their own way back.

No sooner had the boys entered the museum, than the corporals and I headed to the bars in Covent Garden. The balcony of the Punch and Judy was a favourite of mine; it overlooks the street performers doing their acts, and some of them are very talented. A skinful later and we headed back to the imperial war museum to catch the coach.

"I know a shortcut through a park," suggested our Troop Commander who knew the London area well, having served there for a few years in his previous post.

The gate was locked.

"Let's climb over," he said.

"It's a 6 foot fence with steel spikes on top."

"We'll be alright, just jump over," he said.

I was lifted up first and jumped over, putting my arm through the bars to assist lifting up troopy, the one whose idea this was. He suddenly slipped and impaled himself on a spike. I now had one guy on one side of the fence, one guy impaled six feet up on a metal spike and myself stuck inside a locked public garden surrounded by 6ft bloody spikes.

"What now smart arse?" I said.

"Get me off this bloody fence," he replied, clearly in some discomfort at this point.

"One...two...three...up," as we lifted him up and back and he fell back on the opposite side of the fence to me and landed on top of the other guy with a thud. We then made the decision that I would run ahead and meet the coach, while they hobbled off to St. Thomas' Hospital for repairs. After several attempts I managed to climb the fence on the other side of the grounds and met the coach in time.

The heavy traffic meant we arrived back at the Cannon in Chatham just in time for last orders, and already sitting there sipping a pint were my partners in crime, with the injured party displaying a large bandage wrapped around his thigh. He said the spike had gone through to the bone, and that probably stopped it from going right through and out the other side, and impaling him good and proper, which would have made for quite a different story for the Sapper Magazine!

Young soldiers are prone to getting into trouble, most of which either involves an altercation in a pub or club, and usually after a night in the cells they would be handed over to the military to deal with. Other offences like AWOL can go to a Court Martial depending on the length of time the soldier is absent and a sentence of up to 2 years in detention can be imposed.

I often had to deal with soldiers not returning after a weekend or after they have had a few weeks leave. Usually a phone call to their parents or next of kin would persuade them to come back, and they would get whacked with a £50 fine or a slap on the wrist from the old man, but at least they avoided the detention centre.

One individual had been AWOL for months, and the Scottish police had visited his parent's residence several times before they finally caught up with him. He was eventually arrested and released on bail. The military were then informed of his whereabouts, and I was tasked with going to collect him. I was briefed prior to my departure and handed a set of handcuffs.

"Why the handcuffs," I queried.

As a Senior Non-Commissioned Officer, I was given permission to handcuff the soldier to my own wrist until he was back in military custody, a decision I would have to make on the ground at the time. I dread to imagine what customs would think if I got searched at the airport with a pair of handcuffs in my rucksack.

I flew from Heathrow to Dundee the following morning, collected a hire car and agreed to meet him in a pub in the centre of Perth. It was on the relatively short journey to Perth that it suddenly dawned on me, if I was to handcuff the young soldier, how the hell was I supposed to drive back to the airport? Decision made, the handcuffs would stay in the bottom of my rucksack.

I arrived at Perth city centre around midday and parked up in the car park at the back of the pub and made my way into the bar. It was full of punters, and it became immediately apparent that they were the young soldier's family and friends there to support him. Time to be tactful! I raised a hand as a friendly gesture as I made my way over to the young soldier through the crowd and shook his hand.

He introduced me to his family as his troop sergeant, and I felt it right to sit amongst his family and chat for a while as various family members kept offering me a pint every 5 minutes. Tempted as I was, it would have only ended in disaster. Imagine the headlines, 'Sergeant gets pissed while on official duty to apprehend a deserted soldier'.

The young soldier's girlfriend sitting next to him was six months pregnant with their first baby and the family pleaded with me not to take him back. I sympathised with them as I was only recently a father myself and would have hated to have not been there for their birth, but he had to go back with me. I informed them he would be looked after, and I would explain his defence to the commanding officer. In the end, the soldier was sentenced to 3 months detention but was discharged early to be at the birth of his child.

I organised along with my Troop Commander a 2-week adventure training package to Jersey in the Channel Islands; the package was split into two one-week packages with 30 personnel each week accommodated within the small cadet force camp at Les Ormes, situated on the western side of the island. Activities included cave canoeing, rock climbing, water skiing and a beach day, and the weather was fantastic. Organising the trip was the hard part and once on the island the group leaders took their groups, leaving me and my troop commander plenty of spare time to play some golf. I was hoping the spike he had through his leg during our previous exploits in London would have handicapped him a bit more, but unfortunately for me it didn't do anything to his golf swing, and he was a hard man to beat.

In the evenings I laid on a liberty wagon to ferry the guys into St Helier at 7pm and return at 1pm. The guys seemed to be behaving themselves until the weekend came around. I received a phone call on Sunday, "Sergeant Roberts? Good morning, it's the desk Sergeant here from St Helier police station".

Sensing this was not good news, wild imaginings were instantly running through my head - fighting, assault or rape even.

"What's happened?" I said fearing the worst. "I have 2 of your soldiers here in custody." "On my way," I said and hot-footed over to the police station, where the desk Sergeant explained that they had been arrested for urinating in a public place. He said they would have been sent on their way with a verbal warning, but they decided to chops-it-off instead of keeping their big mouths shut, so his police officers nicked them. I sighed with relief and informed the police sergeant that I would ensure such a serious crime would not happen again, and a few words in the soldiers' ears was enough to deter them from becoming serious criminals.

My OC decided to fly over and visit for a few days, putting a slight downer on things. It's always a bit tense when the old man is about, however he brought with him news of my promotion to Staff Sergeant, along with a posting order for me to report to 73 Engineer Regiment (Volunteers) as a Permanent Staff Instructor (PSI), based at Chesterfield. The news of promotion was great, but the Territorials - come on, for fucks sake!

Part 11

CHESTERFIELD 03/05

With no army quarters close by, Clare, my 2 daughters and I were set up in a four bed, detached, rental house near the TA barracks in Chesterfield. I Reported for duty, which was a strange feeling in a unit with no soldiers; just a handful of administrative staff occupying the offices within the small camp. My new boss, the Permanent Staff Administrative Officer, was a grumpy old ex-quartermaster who had served 35 years previously in the Royal Engineers, a retired major with a bark bigger than his bite. Often falling asleep in his chair, normally just after lunch with the motion sensors detecting no movement would automatically turn the lights off in his office. I used to think he had gone out, he would let out a snore waking himself up and the lights would flicker back to life. I would shout through,

"You okay, boss?"

He would reply,

"Yes why?"

"Nothing, just checking you're still alive," I would mumble to myself.

Clare was left at home with the girls while I attended my Regimental Quartermaster Sergeants course, six weeks at Deepcut, when I got the news that she was pregnant again -this time a boy. I was chuffed to bits, but deep down I was thinking, how the bloody hell are we going to afford it? I held a class 1 heavy goods licence and was offered a bit of work on the side, driving for an agency firm in Sheffield, so while Clare was busy doing mum stuff I was driving up and down the M1, two nights a week. One delivery was to a well-known supermarket depot and after they unloaded me, they had left several boxes of sliced salmon on the back. I questioned why they left it and they replied,

"It wasn't on the list mate".

As I made my way back to the depot I remembered a soldier who had recently left the mob; he owned a pub next to the hospital in Chesterfield which served meals. I rang him and we agreed to meet at a service station in a few hours' time. We offloaded the salmon into the boot of his car, and with salmon on his menu for the next few weeks I was able to treat Clare to a free meal and a bottle of wine at the house.

After Luke was born, we decided no more kids and arranged for me to have the snip. Clare and I drove down to Nottingham's sexual health clinic for the procedure. At the reception desk downstairs half a dozen men were sitting and we thought we were in for a long wait. I checked in with the receptionist, giving her my name. She asked "What seems to be the problem?" to which I replied,

"No problem, I'm here for my procedure - the snip".

"Oh, you want to be upstairs. This is the STD clinic." As we turned around to leave we saw half a dozen men lowering their heads in shame.

I was led into a room and the nurse asked me to undress, lay on the bed and she placed a plastic sheet over me. She left the room while I stripped naked and lay on the bed. The sheet had a hole where the operation was to take place. Laying back I pulled my tackle through the hole and waited for the nurse, she walked in followed closely by a female doctor and two female university students. The old nurse pointed at my penis and said, "I don't think you need to have that on show".

Embarrassingly tucking it back through the hole in the sheet, the doctor leaned in holding in her hand a syringe and said, "you're about to feel a small prick!"

My cousin, Phill, would visit as often as he could on weekends. I had 2 mountain bikes with toddler seats attached to the back of the frame, behind the seat. It gave us the perfect excuse to give Clare some time to relax from the girls while Luke slept. With the girls saddled up on the back of the bikes we headed off along the canal paths, stopping off at a few watering holes on the way. After a few beers we approached a narrow section of path when Phill accidentally clipped my back tyre, his bike dropped to one side. The weight of my daughter strapped on the back meant she was now dangling at a 90 degree angle over the canal! All I can say is that it was a good job she was strapped in, disaster averted we decided best to walk the rest of the canal, and bribed the girls with a bag of sweets not to tell mummy.

I popped up to see my fellow PSI in Sheffield for a brew and chat about an up-and-coming joint TA weekend we were arranging, and in the corner of his room was a 6ft stuffed Lion King.

"What the fuck is that, mate?" I said, turning his head, he looked at me like I was stupid.

"Really, who the fuck do you think it is?" he said.

After I'd finished spitting my tea across the room, he went on to tell me he won it in a supermarket raffle, and how he'd had to strap it to the roof of his car, an old Jaguar XJS. He said,

"You thought you looked stupid, you should have seen the funny looks I got driving through Sheffield's town centre".

I was nominated to be the Cadre SNCO for the up and coming JNCO cadre, it was time for a bit of pay back for the bullshit I had been subjected to some 15 years earlier. The TA cadre is only 10 days long as they also have civilian jobs, so impossible for them to do a full 6 weeks. I had 2 infantry Corporals instructors assigned to me to carry out most of the training.

During the second week we were at Chickerell camp in Weymouth, I scheduled to have them a couple of times a week for drill practice. During one of my sessions I took them down onto the bridging hard, final rehearsal for their final pass off parade. I would enjoy a bit of banter with them whilst barking drill order, "LEFT TURN, RIGHT TURN," etc. When one soldier decided to give me a bit of cheek, and thought he'd got away with it.

"RIGHT TURN," I yelled and marched them down the hard, a large concrete ramp used to launch boats into the sea, until they were all knee deep in the water.

I had waited 15 years for this opportunity and said, "Gentlemen, don't fuck with your Cadre Staffy!"

I felt as though I had finally satisfied my revenge for the soaking my Sergeant Major gave me and my fellow JNCOs all those years ago.

Night navigation exercise, and I set them off in pairs, with only the use of a filtered torch and a map. They were spaced out at 10 minute intervals and under the cover of darkness, they had to find 10 reference points over a 5km route; each checkpoint gave the coordinates to the next and so on, but unbeknown to them it was a full circle around the training area's perimeter. Checkpoint 6 was a small wooden hut and once all the soldiers had been set off I made my way over to the hut and waited with a colleague for them to pass through. Multiple white lights and voices began to approach. I waited until they got nearer and then shouted,

"Turn them fucking lights off, and shut the fuck up". Lights quickly started to turn off with muffled voices whispering to each other,

"Shit, is that Staff?"

I called them all into my position and gave them a few more fucks, before telling them to get inside the wooden hut and grab themselves a bacon sandwich. They all said,

"Cheers, Staff".

But soon realising there were no sandwiches, one asked "Where's the bacon sarnies, Staff?".

"Really?" I said, setting them off on their merry way, chuntering as they went.

My colleague and I set off back across the field, hands in our pockets, chatting about how stupid they were to believe we had made them bacon sandwiches. But as we strolled through the farmer's field we walked into an electric fence - Karma's a bitch!

Reserve soldiers were being mobilised to Iraq and Afghanistan while I was at home, playing happy families. Although I understood the career path I was on, I began to question my position within the forces. My prayers may have just been answered when I received a chance phone call from a staff sergeant based in Ripon. He was asking me if I knew of any PSI positions available. He was in his last couple of years and wanted a steady posting which would allow him time to carry out his resettlement process into civvy street. I quickly replied,

"Yes, mine mate".

A selfish decision I made without any consultation with Clare, but I needed to get back into a regular unit on active service. I was getting too comfortable serving in a non-operational unit. We both agreed a job swap and went about putting the wheels in motion, and some weeks later I received a posting order to 38 Engineer Regiment in Ripon.

Part 12

RIPON TO IRAQ

Another house move, and the luxury accommodation we had become accustomed to was over as I crammed my now growing family into a small 3-bedroom semi-detached pads quarter. I joined my squadron who were already training up in Scotland, building and refurbishing bridges. I arrived to find the squadron was living in military tents in the back field of a holiday campsite where I was met by my counterpart, the Squadron Quartermaster Sergeant (SQMS), a big lad who went by the name of 'Pistols'. He was from Barry Island in South Wales, a gentle giant with an infectious nature.

He accommodated me in a small 9 x 9 tent next to his. It was late summer and I was ill-prepared. Applecross sits in a bay opposite the Isle of Raasay in the Inner Hebrides and the first night the temperature plummeted below freezing; with no ground sheet on the old canvas tents the cold permeated up and under my camp bed and ended in long nights freezing my bloody socks off, I was soon wishing I was back in Chesterfield. However, the local pub provided sanctuary from the cold most evenings when the sun went down.

Commandeering a military motorbike from my own transport section, allowed me to visit some of the remote sites not accessible by 4 wheeled vehicles. I spent my days scrambling around the mountains and paying the odd visit to the bridging sites. I met up with the plant staff sergeant whose team was busy upgrading a section of road near the visitor's centre. He asked me if I could move the three ABLE bridging vehicles which had been left parked up by the bridging crew, as they had gone back to Ripon. He held the keys but nobody on site was trained to move them. Handing me the keys, I jumped off my motorbike and headed over to move the vehicles. Moments later there was an almighty crunch, and looking round I saw that a grader had reversed and reduced my mode of transport to scrap - bloody plant operators!

The drive back to Ripon was gruelling. With the vehicles lined up we made an early start, setting off north around Applecross's peninsula early the next morning. A 3.5 tonne weight limit prevented us from driving the shortcut over the pass due to its narrow and steep winding road, adding a further two hours on top of the 400-mile journey. Seats like park benches and rock-hard suspension made the 14 hours numb going.

When we returned to Ripon our Commanding Officer called a briefing and all Officers, WO and SNCO attended; he informed us we had been officially warned off for deployment to Iraq as part of 19 Light Brigade on

Op Telic 9. I guess the one thing that all soldiers fear the most about going to war is not the worry for themselves, but for their families and loved ones they leave behind. I could now see it from both sides of the fence, what with Chris having been involved in the Falklands War. Things now just got a bit more serious as we moved into pre-deployment training. Fitness levels needed to improve as we started more physical endurance training, carrying heavier bergens and equipment to increase our strength and stamina. Weapon handling, range days and nuclear, biological and chemical warfare training was paramount as we knew Saddam Hussein's regime had an arsenal of chemical weapons and he was not afraid to use them.

As our deployment date grew closer, two weeks mandatory pre-deployment training, the first week at Salisbury Plain training area, focused attention on convoy patrols and drills to be carried out if engaged under enemy fire known as "Actions on".

Second week we moved down to Lydd and Hythe firing range in Kent. As well as the physical training we received briefings and updates on real time tactics being used by the Iraqi insurgents, who were becoming more and more sophisticated in their methods as the war progressed. Patient and cunning, they would monitor how our forces conducted foot patrols and vehicle convoy moves, so our own tactics had to evolve to combat these threats.

It was reported an insurgent spent two days crawling on his belly along an air strip in extreme heat to plant explosives that crippled a large military cargo plane carrying vital fuel and rations as it came into land - a very successful hit on our coalition forces by a single insurgent proved how cunning and patient they could be.

The heavily criticised snatch Land Rovers were still being used in theatre; they were modified vehicles with a bulletproof body and windows, and a hatch on the roof which allowed a soldier to pop his head out and provide top cover, allowing a 360 degree arc of fire. I arrived with my troop at one of the training stands, and was briefed on the following scenario -I was to command a snatch Land Rover with its crew and drive down range as if we were part of a mobile patrol in a major city in Iraq. With my crew briefed, we loaded up. My driver and myself in the front and 4 crew members in the back, we set off down the centre of the range. Moments later there was a loud bang, a thunder flash had been thrown by the directing staff simulating a grenade attack. My brief was clear. On hearing the explosion our vehicle would be completely disabled in the ambush, so our drill was to debus, frag the vehicle and firefight away from the kill zone. Fragmentation grenades contain phosphorus and will continue to burn, their purpose is to destroy any sensitive information or equipment the enemy could use to their advantage, mainly our encrypted vehicle's radio equipment.

"Bang"- a thunder flash exploded as electronic targets popped up to our front.

"Debus," I shouted and my crew immediately exited the vehicle and engaged targets.

I popped a smoke grenade under the back of the vehicle to simulate that I had fragged the vehicle. Having already established a Charlie and Delta fire team, I had 3 guys on their bellies engaging the targets to the right of the vehicle and I joined my 2 guys on the left side, a method widely used by the military. As commander I gave the orders to move and in the event of the commander being killed the 2i/c would take control. Charlie fire team gave covering fire while Delta fire team sprinted back a short distance and went to ground to give covering fire for the Delta team to retreat, pepper potting out of the Killzone.

Later, ready to go again, I briefed my second team. We were loading the vehicle as before when I noticed a hole in the dashboard where I had been sitting 15 minutes earlier. A stray bullet was lodged there. I immediately brought this to the attention of the directing staff and could see where the bullet had gone through the bulletproof panel at the back of the vehicle, and through the commander's seat where I had been sitting. It plagued my mind, not only for the safety of our troops in Iraq, but also as I questioned what had really happened to the two Royal Engineer soldiers killed when they were ambushed in a similar snatch vehicle during a routine patrol in 2003. I had been one of the coffin bearers during their repatriation at Brize Norton a few years earlier.

I informed my commanding officer of the issue and he was also shocked, but not surprised. He pushed the matter higher and a few days later the answer from Whitehall was even more shocking - Iraq insurgents use 7.62 mm rounds and although a bigger calibre bullet than our standard 5.56 mm round, it would not penetrate the armour of a snatch Land Rover. I wasn't able to dispel that theory and the answer did not sit well with me. Snatch vehicles were being phased out and being replaced by the foxhound armoured vehicle, but the rollout was still two years off.

Prior to deployment, soldiers with young children have the opportunity to record a reading onto a CD. I dictated my children's favourite book which I used to read to them before bedtime, and my girls, even to this day, remember listening to my recording when I was away. Luke was a bit young to remember but it must have brought some comfort to them during my absence.

I was on the first flight out in November 2006 as part of the first Relief in Place (RIP) and flew from Teesside airport to Abu Dhabi in a civilian charter plane, before being transferred into an RAF C17 Globemaster into Shaibah air base. Shaibah was the UK's logistic base in Iraq until its handover to the Iraqi army at the end of 2007. After two days of briefings and check firing of our personal weapons, we were airlifted by Merlin helicopter under the cover of nightfall into Basra Air Station.

The RIP is designed to bed in new troops alongside the outgoing troops over a short period of time to allow for continuity; it allows the first boots on the ground to get to know and understand their surroundings alongside their experienced counterparts prior to their return home. The Iraqi insurgents would know when the RIP was happening and would increase their attacks on the base, knowing the base was at its most vulnerable time. Within two days of arriving at Basra the mortar attacks increased; within the first month we were being hit on average 15 times a day.

A mortar's effective range depends on varying factors, the size of mortar tube being used is one; the insurgents normally fired portable weapons in 2 to 3 man teams, using a lightweight mortar tube mounted on a tripod. The mortar round was dropped down the tube with the mortar's flight path and operating range being altered depending on the angle of the tube.

The insurgents knew the camp was built around Basra's airport and would fire mortars from a few kilometres away using the airport's tower as their point of reference, adjusting their aim slightly left or right in their hope of hitting a Corimec office, a kitchen or accommodation tents, to inflict maximum devastation. Each tent on the base housed up to 8 men and during our time, each bed space was allocated enough high-density blocks to give a 3 high layer of surrounding wall, the blocks look like household breezeblocks, but five times heavier to give additional protection from any mortars landing close by, hence why our bed spaces were aptly named coffins.

Many of us did away with our cot beds and opted to sleep on a thin mattress on the floor to be nearer the ground and next to the high-density blocks, in the hope of being offered more protection if a mortar was to land close by. One early evening I was sitting chatting to Pistols when the tell-tale sound of a mortar round whistled overhead, exploding close to our tent. I dived for cover in the walkway between our coffins with Pistols landing on top of me. Shrapnel from the blast had ripped through parts of the tent. Shortly after the barrage of mortars and explosions stopped, you allow a soak period of around 15 minutes in case of any more incoming, but usually the insurgents have long gone before they are detected. Turning to Pistols I said, "I know we should wait a bit longer mate, but do you mind getting the fuck off me, you fat lump". He replied in his South Wales accent, "I do love a good cwtch", a Welsh term for cuddle.

Happy to be still alive and still being able to make light of the situation is a squaddies coping mechanism.

Morning routine was always the same, get up around 06:00, do phys for an hour, grab a quick shower, get some breakfast, and head off to work. To get to my office, a portacabin over by the vehicle park, I had to pass an aviary which housed around 40 small birds. Why someone had opted to build an aviary on a military camp was anyone's guess, but every morning they would all chirp and follow me along the length of their enclosure until I had passed. One morning after I had been there about a week I noticed the aviary had fallen silent. Turns out the person responsible for them was an Iraqi employee who had not returned to work for whatever reason and it meant the poor little buggers went without food and water and died. I felt sick.

A visit to the camp barber was a very nerve-wracking experience; for $10 you got to sit in a chair staring at the mirror at a local Iraqi setting about your head with a pair of scissors and a cutthroat razor whilst listening to shite music being played on local radio.

Three days before Christmas I received orders to prepare five Demountable Rack Offload and Pick up Systems vehicles (DROPS) for an up and coming op. My orders were to load them with modified shipping containers to be used as crowd control obstacles, an effective system first used in Northern Ireland during the troubles. Bracing struts were welded and mounted on the side to allow the doors to be braced open once deployed on the ground, providing an extended barrier.

My team and I were being integrated with the main battle group on this up-and-coming mission. I set about preparing the containers and carried out initial training according to the limited information l had so far received. I later attended the main briefing - the mission was being headed by a major from the 1st Battalion of the Staffordshire

Regiment and two SAS operators. Our mission was to take over a large police compound in the Al Jameat region of the city to stop the torture and killing of prisoners by the renegade Iraqi police officers, and to demolish the site to avoid any reestablishment in the future.

At 22:00 hours on Christmas Eve the battlegroup lined up as we waited for the order to move. The convoy was made up mainly of warrior tanks, armoured personnel carriers, and my team of DROPS vehicles, which offered very little armoured protection. An Apache helicopter was to provide overwatch as we moved out from the airport to the edge of the city. At approximately 02:00 we entered the city, our vehicles' lights switched to convoy, a tactical mode immobilising all lights including brake lights and indicators except for a small torch-like light at the rear of each vehicle, allowing the vehicle behind to follow. My driver's face was pinned up against the windscreen straining his eyes to keep the warrior tank in sight. The poorly lit street lamps along the main road leading into the city gave some relief, a very quiet and eerie feeling as we entered the city. I had two personal role radios (PRR), one to communicate with my team and a command radio which was now alive with chatter. A voice came over the radio,

"Around 100 insurgents believed to be at the police station armed with small arms weapons".

Radio chatter increased as our convoy started to take incoming fire from our flank, which our escort warrior to our front soon dispatched. The tell-tale trail of a Rocket Propelled Grenade (RPG) round flew past our window; this shit just got real. I was feeling extremely vulnerable in a vehicle with very little protection. The Kevlar bucket seat offered some protection from any roadside bombs, and a Kevlar plate slid across the door protected us from small arms fire from the side, but the only protection from the front was a metal grill used in riot situations as protection from bricks and stones. I sank as low as possible, praying my Kevlar helmet would extend down over my knees. Unable to return fire due to the metal grillage over the windows and Kevlar protection, all my faith was in the protection force, but even if I could have, I would have been foolish to try without night vision goggles and a restricted firing position.

The 100 insurgents soon dispersed on hearing the Apache helicopter above and the thundering sound of the approaching warriors put the fear of God into them. They knew full well the capabilities of the Apache helicopter and were wise to have legged it. Ploughing through the compound wall our Combat Engineer Tractor punched a hole for the Armoured Personnel Carriers carrying troops to access into the compound. Warrior tanks surrounded the area as my team prepared to position our barriers across the main access roads. But then a call came over the radio to me to "stand down". I was a bit gutted to be honest as we were led into the compound. Instructing my team to remain with the vehicles I entered the police station to assist the protection force. We released the prisoners and led them out of the crammed and overcrowded cells. The smell, and the human waste overflowing from a toilet in the corner made me retch; the conditions these poor people had been made to live in was shocking. They had been beaten, starved and were in a serious state of malnutrition, some in a crippled state as I helped them onto the waiting trucks.

The Military Police were there to gather intelligence, collecting computers and paperwork while our sappers got busy rigging the police station with explosives. The morning 172 daylight provided a sense of our surroundings and we saw a police car parked next to the building. It seemed a waste for it to go up in smoke. I looked around for the keys to no avail. The order came around 09:00am to move out. Clear of the compound, a young sapper was given the privilege of detonating the explosive charge - the explosion was so powerful our 15 tonne DROPS vehicle shook as civilians wandering the streets fell to the floor.

Iraqis picked themselves up and carried on going about their business, the streets were bustling as we made our way out of the city, and again we were fired upon by small arms fire, insurgents taking pot shots hoping for a result. I saw one of our squadron's Fijian sappers, who was top cover in the vehicle in front of me, place a well-aimed shot and the shooter went down; he was the seventh insurgent to lose his life on that mission.

Out of the city our route took us through the Rumaila oil fields, a long detour back to base to avoid insurgents second guessing our route and to avoid any improvised explosive devices planted along the way. It was now midday; the desert sands and the burning flames from the oil fields increased the humidity, and there I witnessed a lone man in the distance miles from anywhere standing in an oil spill with a bucket, and covered in oil. I have no idea what he was doing there, I saw no vehicle and it was such a powerful image that sticks in my mind whenever I think of my time in Iraq.

The Welsh opera singer, Katherine Jenkins, was in Iraq visiting the troops as part of The Combined Services Entertainment (CSE). I happened to be in the right place at the right time! I was sitting alone having a late lunch when the OC along with his entourage including Kathrine entered the cook house. It was relatively quiet and he spotted me and fair play brought her over to my table and introduced me as a fellow Welshy. I stood up and introduced myself as she sat next to me and had lunch. I don't think I can call it a date, but if anyone asks, I'll definitely take it.

I was later summoned to the CO's office. Shit! What's going on? The Regimental Sergeant Major gave me some bullshit story about how I'd fucked up. I was bewildered as the CO shouted to me to enter his office. Also there was Pistols, and as I was handed a small glass of port he congratulated us both for being selected for promotion to Warrant Officer Class 2; a dinner date with Kathrine Jenkins and promotion all on the same day - I was doing okay for a kid from Wales.

Normally after a promotion you were posted to another unit within the corps, so I was chuffed when the CO had already assigned me within the same unit, and informed me I would take up the position from the outgoing Regimental Quartermaster Sergeant Technical (RQMS(T) when we returned to the UK, a position in which I would be responsible for managing the unit's technical equipment - my days of being in charge of a body of men was now over.

But it was still a few months until our end of tour and the prospects of me going home to be promoted and see my family early would have to wait. One of the hardships of being on operations is dealing with the phone calls home. I'd try to phone home at least once a week to reassure my family I was doing okay. I remember speaking to my children, and my girls would tell me about their day in school and about their friends, which was always nice to hear, but during one particular phone call my son said,

"I miss you Dad. When will you be home?"

The tone of his voice hit an emotional nerve, I really missed them, too, and as I hung up the phone I couldn't contain the tears and the emotions I was feeling. I went to a quiet spot and had a cry - I just wanted to hug my kids.

I was soon due R&R; two weeks back home with my family. Excitedly, I made my way down to departure, a large tent by the side of the runway with low lighting. Our R&R party clambered on board an RAF C130 Hercules transporter for our flight to Qatar. Take-off would be under the cover of darkness with no runway or plane lights to give any sign of a take-off. We began taxing down the runway when the plane stopped suddenly.

"Debus, debus!" the loadmaster shouted, opening the rear ramp of the plane. The sound of incoming mortars landing in the distance, as we scrambled down the ramp and dived to the tarmac. Soldiers lay scattered across the runway as we waited for the incoming mortars to silence, and for the all clear and to be called back on board. After a short soak period of around 5 minutes the loadmaster screamed,

"Get back on board," and bodies bumped into each other as we rushed to get back to our seats. The last man on, the loadmaster radioed the pilot and the plane began to taxi as soon as the ramp started to rise. I could feel the plane make its final turn as he lined up on the main runway as the ramp door finally closed. Without a pause the roar of the huge propellers increased sharply as we set off down the runway. A short take off and we were ascending steeply as the pilot fired hundreds of flares in our wake; heated chaff propellants filled the sky to divert any heat seeking missiles which may have been fired during our ascent.

Clear of Iraqi airspace we were soon landing safely at the American Air Force Base in Qatar, only to be informed that our onward civilian flight to Teesside would be delayed by up to 48 hours. This would be lost time with our families. "Great, any fucking good news?" I muttered to myself, as I'm sure many others on the flight were thinking. Facilities on the base included a 24 hour cook house, a duplex cinema, a swimming pool and a bar, a gleam of hope I thought; however we were informed that all visitors to the base were limited to two beers a day. Beer tokens could be obtained from the bedding store once you'd signed for your mattress.

"What twat thought of that idea?" one lad said, echoing the thoughts of every man in the room.

It was extremely hot in Qatar, far hotter than Iraq, and I was unable to sleep in the stifling accommodation block. The canopy over the outside bar provided some shelter from the blistering sun. Having drunk my allocation for the day we soon cottoned on to a way of getting more beer tokens, and by the end of the day I had signed for five sets of bedding but the journey to and fro from the bedding store was a grind. However, the extra beer tokens made it worthwhile!

The cookhouse was amazing, an all-inclusive style food festive: steak, fish, burgers, a salad bar, even an ice cream parlour for fuck sakes. Apart from the alcohol restriction those few days were like being in a holiday camp - even the

RAF don't get it that good. All joking aside though, the Americans certainly know how to look after their troops.

It felt strange being at home as I tried to adjust to a normal family routine, having spent time dodging mortars only a few days earlier. Now here I was shopping in a supermarket, listening to people complain about their 3G network. No sooner you start to adjust to normality and your anxiety about returning back to Iraq and the thought of being away from your family creeps in. As a military man those times spent with your family are precious. The morning I was due to fly back the postman delivered a letter with NS&I stamped on the envelope. With hopes of a big premium bond win I ripped open the envelope; maybe I won't need to go back? But any hope of staying home soon diminished - all I'd won was £50 quid.

I was soon back in Iraq and attending my Command, Leadership and Management course, a must do course to gain my substantive promotion, and consequently any further promotion, and also equally important to qualify for a Warrant Officer's pension. The course included topical debates, leadership skills and global political issues in which we had each being given a 45-minute topic to present. I was allocated East Timor, and with no idea of the country's issues, I set about gathering as much information as I could, ready to present in two days' time. I must admit, I found it a bit stressful.

Regular tea breaks helped destress, and the dozen or so candidates on the course would gather outside in the warm sun with a brew and a bit of banter. Suddenly one of the lads let out a yelp and the six-foot two, war-hardened infantry soldier jumped on a nearby bench to take refuge from a camel spider that had crept up in his shadow to seek shelter from the sun. Now exposed to the sunlight the large critter, the size of an adult's hand, provided a moment of light entertainment as all twelve of us joined the man on the table.

The simplest of things can amuse a bored soldier. Tony Blair, the Prime Minister, paid a visit. We all gathered round to listen to his drivel; the BBC news correspondent sat on a plastic chair on the back of a flatbed truck, and with the camera rolling we began to rock the vehicle back and forth as he broadcast to the nation. The Prime Minister started his walkabout, shaking hands with the troops and telling us what a marvellous job we were doing. Pistols leaned across, grabbing the PM's hand and introduced himself as the Mayor of Barry, to which the PM responded,

"Really?"

Pistols replied,

"Do you think I'd be standing here if I was?"

Priceless!

It was late evening when we finally arrived in coaches back in Ripon, no welcome party as I grabbed my belongings off the coach and made the 10 minute walk home. The kids were already asleep when I popped my head into their bedroom and kissed their foreheads as they slept. Next morning I woke to pandemonium and at first I thought we were getting mortared, until I realised I was home. But it was just my kids screaming and shouting at the end of the bed, followed by a flood of tears. It is the greatest feeling after several months away.

Part 13

NORTHERN IRELAND TO AFGHANISTAN

The difficult task of a unit move now lay ahead, the main driving force being that the move fell to the QM's department which I was now part of. For the next 6 months I set about planning and coordinating the vehicle and load manifest for the ferry bookings of over 200 vehicles and trailers. I was to move my family across the water earlier than the rest of the regiment in preparation for receiving each ferry load and escort them in from Larne ferry terminal to Massereene barracks to ensure a smooth transition. But prior to this, the Warrant Officer (WO) and Sergeants' Mess arranged a trip to a comedy club in Liverpool. We arrived around 3pm and the organiser arranged for us to split into small groups of 4, handing us a question sheet he said all the answers to these questions lay inside a pub. After many questions were answered and several pints of beer later we eventually arrived at the club. After a great night of entertainment we piled back onto the coach for the 2- hour drive back to Ripon, crossing the Pennines around midnight. With no toilet on the coach we pleaded with the driver to pull over; 50 guys now stood in one long line and like a military drill move, we proceeded to empty our bladders - with the wind in our faces we may well have just stayed on the coach!

Our family quarters were around a 15-minute drive away at RAF Aldergrove, and as soon as the regiment was settled, we received orders to deploy on operations again, this time to Afghanistan on Op Herrick 10. Training once again stepped up, only this time my role as a Warrant Officer was to support the unit's needs and provide the squadrons with the operational equipment they would need. Ammunition demands were hitting my desk daily as troops were carrying out live firing at the Ballykinler ranges, and as equipment was being shipped in, I had the mundane job of dividing it evenly amongst the troops.

Deployment date grew closer, and each unit within our brigade went through its Op Herrick training prior to departure. All troops deploying to Afghanistan had to attend a specially designed training facility designed to emulate a Forward Operating Base (FOB). FOB bases were spread around Helmand province where UK forces operated and they often came under attack from the Taliban. Our boys had to be ready and able to hold their defensive position without being overrun so pre-training was key.

I arrived in Afghanistan as part of the pre-advanced party, along with six others, including our commanding officer, to take over key positions from 3 commando brigade on Op Herrick 9. After a 48 hr delay at Kandahar air base we were eventually flown in a Merlin helicopter to Camp Bastion on the 6th of March 2009.

A temporary telephone was set up next to my bed for comms to our Ops room back in Antrim. During the early hours of the 8th of March I received a phone call from a fellow Warrant Officer back home in Northern Ireland informing me of a major incident, and could I fetch the CO urgently. I immediately jumped out of my sleeping bag and ran down the corridor of our tented accommodation and woke the boss.

"Sir, there's an urgent call from back home, something serious has happened but he wouldn't tell me."

I stood next to him as he was informed of the shooting outside our barracks at Massereene. of Sappers Patrick Azimkar (21) and Mark Quincy (23). They were killed and 4 others were injured while collecting pizzas off a delivery driver outside the front gate. The horrific news of their deaths on the eve of their departure to Afghanistan was not only a huge blow to our unit about to deploy on operations, but utterly devastating for their families.

On the arrival of the main body at Camp Bastion, a vigil was held to say a few words for the two of our young soldiers whose lives had been cut short by two cowardly members of the IRA, in such a cruel and gutless way.

We had to stay focused, and it was necessary to establish a routine. I, personally, focused on my phys and it started with a 5-kilometre run at 05:00 every morning before the sun got too hot. With my routine well and truly established another fellow Warrant Officer asked if he could join me, so we sat down one evening and put a varied training plan together which included gym work and weights. We agreed to get up every morning at 05:00 hours, six times a week and we allocated ourselves one rest day. Next morning, I woke him up at around 05:00. He rolled over and said,

"Can we call today our rest day".

Our training plan never got started, and I resumed running by myself.

My position as RQMS(T) meant I was grounded in the relative safety of Camp Bastion for the duration of the tour - a camp rat as it's better known. Overhearing a conversation between the OC and 2i/c about a shortage of manning for the next Convoy Logistic Patrol (CLP) to resupply the FOBs caught my attention - a chance to escape for a few days. CLPs normally have a three day turnaround and are a means of providing our brave young men and women with much needed supplies, including letters and parcels from home. Living conditions in an FOB was pretty tough so a message from home provided them with a real morale boost.

"I'll go," I said, jumping into their conversation. "Give me a break from camp". My request was met with some hesitation before the OC replied,

"I can't take the risk of sending you". But he was acutely aware I was suffering from cabin fever and in the end he allowed me to go. I reported to the CLP briefing along with around 80 other soldiers who would make up the patrol of drivers and escorts. I was willing to be an escort and provide top cover in the event of any Taliban attack. After the briefing we gathered under a large shaded area, my rank was of no importance to me at this point; I just wanted to be one of the boys for a few days.

"When I call out your name along with a vehicle registration number, make your way into the opposite shaded area," the CLP SNCO said.

It was a bit like being back in school, when the two football team captains called you out from a line-up into their team, and the last person asked to join them was either overweight or had two left feet. The number of soldiers in my shaded area was getting smaller and smaller until I was the only one left. Now I've never been overweight, and I don't have two left feet, but the major in charge thanked me for wanting to go, but he didn't think it right for a Warrant Officer to come along when they had enough soldiers. I was gutted.

The following week, due to numbers a fellow warrant officer and staff sergeant from our unit went out on the next CLP and drove their DROPS vehicles over a VIED (Vehicle Incendiary Explosive Device). Anticipating the news of their condition back at Camp Bastion we were all fearing the worst. It was hours before we got the news that although their vehicle was a mess they were lucky to have only suffered minor bumps and bruises -the Kevlar underplates saved their lives. As soon as we were certain of the good news, we set about placing auction signs with their names on by the main entrance to the accommodation, for them to see on their return - "Kit for Sale" and then a line crossed through it with the words "Cancelled"!

A major offensive was about to be launched - Op Panchai Palang, otherwise known as Panther's Claw. Its aim was to secure and take control of various canal and river crossings and establish a lasting International Security Assistance Force (ISAF) presence.

A message had come through to the Ops cell to the duty NCO, and he relayed it to the RSM, that one of our boys had been shot in the leg whilst getting out of a helicopter. The RSM immediately went to the hospital, and waited 2 hours for his arrival. By now he was getting anxious and concerned for the soldiers welfare so he went back to the Ops cell to find out if there was any more information. The now sheepish duty NCO had misunderstood the information he had received - apparently the Sapper in question had only twisted his ankle getting out of the helicopter and not been shot by the Taliban as he had first thought. It was no surprise to the RSM - this was the guy who had just bought a boat off eBay for £500 and told everyone he was looking forward to sailing his family around the Isle of Wight.

I prayed the boat came with a paddle and a puncture repair kit for the sake of his family.

It was my 40th birthday. I received parcels from home and the lads had managed to persuade the chefs in the cookhouse to bake me a cake. In army terms I was seen as knocking on a bit. That evening the RSM produced a small bottle of whiskey and we both sat out back of our tent, and drank the whole bottle, deep shit if we were caught, but it's not every day you get to celebrate your 40th in a war zone.

Tour over, we returned to Northern Ireland, our heads held high as we paraded the streets of Antrim as a united front to honour the fallen from our enemies both domestic and abroad, and more importantly to thank our families and friends who stood by us during our tour, and for making the trip over from the mainland to welcome us home – it's what makes a soldier proud to do what he is doing.

Part 14

END OF SERVICE

My finest hour - I was called up to the CO office where I was met by the RSM who ushered me into the boss's office. I had that same feeling I had a few years earlier when in Iraq, I had been selected for promotion to Warrant Officer Class 1, the highest rank a soldier can achieve within the rank and file of the British Army.

A posting shortly followed, and I was appointed Regimental Military Transport Warrant Officer (RMTWO) to 23 Airborne Engineer Regiment, Woodbridge in Suffolk.

Our married quarters sat on the edge of Rendlesham Forest, famous for the alleged UFO encounter in 1980 back when the base was occupied by the American USAF. I was responsible for the regiment's vehicle fleet and vehicle licensing, a dull and boring task. I took up the opportunity to reward my family with the trip of a lifetime to New Zealand to visit Martin, and for the first time our families met. Life was a dream until mid-way through our month-long trip I received the awful news from my eldest brother, Michael - he informed me that Al had been diagnosed with lung cancer. I refused to believe it; although Mike had no reason to lie, I just kept thinking, how could this be? He was one of the fittest men I knew!

I went to visit him on my return and as we sat having a few drinks before he was due to start his chemotherapy, he said to me,

"Don't worry, I'll beat this".

He was a fighter and I believed him. We kept in touch regularly by phone during his treatment until I managed to get up to Wales again. I was shocked - it had only been a few months since I saw him last, but he had lost so much weight and I could see the treatment was taking its toll on him. However, he remained strong.

A few months passed and he was taken into hospital. I spoke to him over the phone; his speech was broken, and his breathing laboured. I told him I would travel up to see him that weekend. I will always regret that I didn't jump into the car and drive to Wales there and then.

Two days later I entered the house after my morning run, and the kids were getting ready for school when I noticed I had 7 missed calls from Al's phone. I phoned back and his wife, Sue, answered - the tone in her voice broke me as she said,

"He's gone, Kev".

The opportunity to commission was on the table but after 26 years' service to Queen and Country my heart was no longer in the game. I decided to call last orders on a career I loved, with all its ups and downs and the emotional roller-coaster ride I wouldn't have changed for anything. I had worked my way up from a young sapper with no clue about life outside of Wales to the dizzy heights of Warrant Officer Class 0ne. It educated me and took me to places I never knew existed. I met some great people along the way, both military and civilian, and the memories I have will last me my lifetime.

I lost the Passion for Life

Several years have passed since my demob from the forces, and I was in a new chapter in my life. My family was settled and I tried to muddle along in civilian life. After a few jobs I found myself bored and unsettled; I secretly wanted my old life back. Civilian life was not what I had expected and as time went on I found myself struggling with the mundane day to day aspects of my new life. I couldn't wait to finish work on a Friday and crack open a bottle of chilled beer as soon as I walked in the house; there were usually 2 crates in the fridge and 2 crates as backup. Headphones on I would listen to music, sometimes I would go right through until the early hours of Sunday, just nodding in and out of sleep before cracking open another bottle. I always made sure I cleared all the empty bottles which would be littered all over the kitchen breakfast bar, before my kids came down for breakfast, and then I would quietly stumble around in the back garden trying to hide the evidence in the recycle bin, shushing the early morning birds now chirping away, as I attempted to put dozens of empty bottles in the recycle box quietly.

The truth was, I was struggling, my head was a mess, and my life slowly began to fall apart. I bottled up whatever was going on inside my head. My bravado got the better of me in the end, suicidal thoughts started to creep in and eventually my marriage broke down and we soon divorced.

My closest family members suspected I was not right, and looking back I should have listened. Instead I was willing to lose everything. Jade and Cayla had gone to university, and I was forced to sell our family home. Clare moved on with Luke and I moved back to Wales with my Mum. Suicidal thoughts ever present and still unable to talk about my struggles, my mum showed me a catalogue of photo albums from my days in the military before the digital age took hold. I used to come home on leave in the 80s and 90s; I was a single soldier then and as well as dropping off my bag of laundry I would hand her some 35mm camera rolls containing pictures from wherever I had been. Unbeknown to me she had developed them and placed the photos in albums. We sat for hours browsing through years of old photographs, and memories came flooding back as I talked about my experiences. She was quite fascinated and interested, and obviously biased, she commented that I should think about writing a book.

Almost immediately I started to put pen to paper. The suicidal thoughts began to fade as I found the process therapeutic and calming, and I spent several hours a day writing as old memories came flooding back as I used the old photos as reference to my experiences.

Thank you for reading my story!

ACKNOWLEDGEMENTS

I would like to thank my dear old mam for taking me in during my hour of need and taking care of me during my lowest time, and without whom I would not have written this book. I owe her a debt of gratitude.

To my Auntie Syl for listening constantly, giving advice, and for providing a sneaky cold beer while we sat in the warm sun of her back garden putting the world to rights.

My 3 children Jade, Cayla and Luke, have been a pleasure to raise, and I am very proud of them and their achievements and for providing me with their reassurance when I needed it most, as without them I would not be here today.

To all my family members including Clare, who have supported me over the last couple of years, especially my cousin Phill and my nephew Nathan. Their continued friendship and constant communication has kept things real and they have been my pillars of support.

To my mucker, George, with whom I served for a few years, and who went through a similar ordeal and remains a good friend.

A special thank you to Sue for giving me her blessing to dedicate this book to her late husband, and my old army buddy Al, and to her brother Andy, a long-time friend who has also taken the time to support me.

Printed in Great Britain
by Amazon

34786915R00126